KNOW THE LANDSCAPE

Roads, Tracks and their Interpretation

KNOW THE LANDSCAPE

Roads, Tracks and their Interpretation

Brian Paul Hindle

B.T. BATSFORD LTD · LONDON

To John

© Brian Paul Hindle 1993

First published 1993

Typeset by Best-set Typesetter Ltd, Hong Kong
and printed in Great Britain by
The Bath Press, Avon

Published by B.T. Batsford Ltd
4 Fitzhardinge Street, London W1H 0AH

A CIP catalogue record for this book is
available from the British Library

ISBN 0 7134 6598 0

Contents

Illustrations

Acknowledgements

Without doubt my greatest debt is to Gustav Dobrzynski, now the sole cartographer in the Department of Geography, University of Salford, for his continuing artistry in producing so many excellent maps for this book; 32 of his 37 maps in this volume are new. The map collections of both the Salford and Manchester Geography Departments provided several of the original map extracts.

The Salford department has continued to support my researches, and I am grateful to Professor Barrie Gleave for his encouragement. As an historical geographer, I am always a little wary when venturing into more recent periods, and Dr Richard Knowles was kind enough to read Chapter 10 (twice!) and made many valuable comments.

The photos were all taken by the author, with the sole exception of Fig. 115; I am grateful to Peter Thornton for allowing me to use this photograph from his book *Lakeland from the Air* (1985).

Harry Margary of Lympne Castle, Kent, who produces many reproductions of early maps, has kindly allowed me to use five extracts, and I am equally grateful to Rex C. Russell of Barton on Humber for permission to use three of his redrawn Lincolnshire enclosure maps, and to Tony Phillips of Keele University for the use of a map from his commentary on the Yates' map of Staffordshire, 1775.

For once I cannot claim that some poor typist has had to struggle with my pencil draft; technology (Amstrad) has come to the rescue!

But at the end of the day, any errors of fact, undue emphasis, or omissions in the text are the responsibility of the author alone.

Preface

The English countryside today bears witness to centuries of human activity and interference in numerous ways that can be interpreted by the informed observer using the skills of the archaeologist and the local historian. This new, wide-ranging series looks at the development of the landscape in Britain and examines the forces at work which have shaped its changing appearance from prehistoric times to the present day.

Each book takes a characteristic aspect of the landscape – such as the estates, monasteries, roads, canals and railways, traces its history and development, explains its function and studies its impact on the landscape throughout history. The subjects are popular and may have easily recognizable features that can still be visited and enjoyed, but some of the effects they have had on the landscape of today are subtle and unexpected and their influence has profoundly changed the look of the countryside around us.

For instance, castles and manor houses are still visible, but so too, to the trained eye, are their fishponds and kitchen gardens, long since demolished or destroyed above ground. What are the reasons behind barely discernible ditches and banks; why is an ancient track just where it is; why were certain villages deserted; less obviously, even why are some trees shaped the way they are? These are some of the intriguing questions discussed in this series.

The authors show how the techniques of landscape research can be used by anyone to enable them to recognize and decipher the signs of various periods of the human past in their own environment. They also guide the reader to some of the sources of documentary evidence and point out particular areas of research that can still be pursued, enabling the individual to make a real contribution.

The series builds up to present a new insight into familiar views and landscapes and brings out some of the hidden features of the British countryside.

1 Introduction

The British landscape as it appears today has evolved over the ten thousand years that have elapsed since the last retreat of the glaciers. Within a few thousand years, a new climax vegetation had established itself, and most of Britain was covered by dense deciduous forest. But about six thousand years ago people capable of adapting and altering the landscape appeared, and started the long process of landscape change that has continued ever since.

One of the crucial elements in changing the landscape has been the creation of tracks and roads, for without them, people would not have been able to trade or exchange goods, populations and towns would not have grown and agriculture and industry would not have flourished. Four very different examples will illustrate how important roads have always been in Britain's economic development. First, prehistoric tracks allowed stone axes to be traded throughout the country; second, the Romans imposed their roads in order to defend this part of their northern frontier; third, medieval towns were established principally in order to trade, and most of the goods were carried by road; and fourth, the increasingly complex agricultural and industrial systems of early modern Britain required the efficient movement by road of goods, people and mail.

Thus throughout history, roads have been fundamental in allowing and promoting economic growth, and they have always provided the backbone of the transportation system.

But roads did not come first; they developed alongside other features in the economy and landscape in a classic 'chicken and egg' relationship. Roads and tracks are important in that they have allowed virtually every other feature of the landscape to develop, and have themselves developed because of those features. Individual elements of the landscape, such as forts and castles, towns and villages, monasteries and churches, estates and parks, mines and mills, woods and fields (many of which are or will be the subject of volumes in this series) all required roads in order to be created and to function effectively. Yet roads are an important feature of the landscape in their own right.

How many roads there are, and how important each is in relation to the others, are determined by the levels of population and economic activity, often influenced by personal and political decisions. Precisely which route each road adopts is partly controlled by the landscape through which it has to pass, and by the level of technology available (i.e. the means of transport and, if the road was being built, road-building techniques). All these factors are significant whether the road being studied is the Roman Watling Street across the English Midlands, or a simple packhorse track snaking its way across the Pennines.

An important distinction has to be

made between those roads which were deliberately planned and built, and those which came into being simply through the continual passage of people and animals. The latter essentially made and maintained themselves, and (apart from the Roman roads) were the norm until the turnpikes were built from the mid-eighteenth century. Moreover, roads undergo a continual process of change in response to the changing needs for them; for example, the Roman road network did not remain the same throughout the four hundred years of Roman rule.

It seems rather strange, therefore, that there are so few books about roads which go beyond simple (and often drab) descriptions of routes and dates; much of the Roman road literature falls into this category. Other books are dusty texts concentrating on the legal aspects of roads, whilst yet others deal with related topics such as travel, travellers, conveyances, conditions on the roads and road-builders.

Many economic history books talk glibly about the growth of trade and industry, but totally ignore the routes along which the goods were carried. Indeed, the study of the history of roads in the context of economic growth has been especially slight. In terms of particular types of roads, those built by the Romans have received much attention, but there is really very little written about such obvious topics as drove roads or turnpikes. Canals and railways, on the other hand, have received exhaustive treatment, with rather more books dealing with their relationship to the economy and the industrial revolution, and with their impact on the landscape.

In terms of landscape development, there are numerous county-level studies which largely ignore the development of their road systems. For some areas, such as Derbyshire, the Lake District, Wessex, the Yorkshire Dales, Dartmoor and parts of Wales, the roads have received varying levels of study, but there are still no good integrated road histories for most parts of Britain. In an age of increasing leisure and travel it is all the more surprising that this should be so. There is surely a good commercial market for well-researched books on the roads of areas such as Kent, Cornwall, the Cotswolds or the Scottish Highlands. Many visitors drive around from one tourist honey-pot to the next, admiring this, photographing that, but ignoring the fascinating history of the very routes along which they travel.

One reason for this neglect is certainly that roads are such a commonplace feature of the landscape that they are taken for granted. Anyone travelling from one place to another in most parts of Britain will find a road or track, and the only problems will be whether to travel by foot, bicycle, bus or car, how long it will take and how much it will cost. In less developed or more mountainous parts of the world, the importance of roads (especially when they are poor, or do not exist at all) is better realized.

The *aim* of this book is threefold: first, to recount the history of the roads of Britain; second, to place that story in the contexts of economic development and landscape change; and third, to give guidelines for further research.

This book cannot hope to give complete coverage of all the roads and tracks of Britain. It is simply impossible to mention, let alone detail, more than a few of the roads of each type in a single volume. The examples which are given are just that, intended to outline the general principles, so that roads elsewhere can be compared with them, and put into a wider context. Equally, some important exceptions to general rules are mentioned, but the reader should always be prepared for individual examples not to follow the general pattern. This book will have been successful if readers want to ask questions about the origins of roads in areas which they know or visit, go and search out the library evidence, and then get out into the countryside to follow particular roads.

This book is not concerned with the urban roads or suburban streets of the last hundred years or so; their history is easily traced on the larger scale Ordnance Survey maps. However, it should always be remembered that all our towns and villages have grown over what was once open countryside, and their growth may have been controlled by the existence of former tracks which have long since vanished. The sheer scale of urban growth has destroyed the physical remains of many old roads, though they too can usually be traced on old maps.

The *approach* adopted is basically chronological, starting with the ancient trackways, and working through to the motorways. But it will soon become very obvious that most roads and tracks do not belong solely to one particular period. For example, many of the earliest trackways were no doubt subsequently used by the Romans, by medieval traders, later by drovers, and some have now been made into long-distance footpaths. Yet there are a few single-period roads, for example Roman roads which have not been used since the departure of the Romans, eighteenth-century military roads soon abandoned, or mine tracks leading to derelict mines; however, these are in the minority. A handful of road types do not fit easily into this system and these 'unusual' roads are dealt with in a separate chapter. The main value of a chronological approach is that it allows a view of both when particular types of road or track were created or first came into use, and how the road network grew and changed. It is important to remember that roads have to be studied as a system rather than as individual routes, for they rarely functioned as the latter.

This is not a guide book, and thus no map references are given; however, there is always enough detail given for individual examples to enable that route to be followed on the appropriate 1:50,000 or 1:25,000 Ordnance Survey maps. Numerous illustrations are provided, including both old and specially drawn maps, and photographs. In any case, roads are such a commonplace feature, that virtually everyone has seen plenty of examples of most types of road; though whether they have understood what they are seeing, in particular when, how and why those roads came into existence is another matter. The author of this book hopes to provide some enlightenment.

Anyone with an enquiring mind, and a bit of time, inclination and energy can help to increase our knowledge and understanding of the development of British roads and tracks. The best possible result of the publication of this book would be the writing of new studies, whether at parish, county or regional level; they might deal only with one particular historical period, or with a particular type of road; or they might attempt a complete integrated road/economic/landscape history of an area. Much remains to be done.

Sources

The available sources for each type of road are mentioned throughout the book, but it is useful to give a brief outline here. They fall into three categories: documents, maps and evidence in the field.

A vast range of *documents* may mention roads or travel. Anglo-Saxon charters and medieval grants often mention roads as boundaries, later itineraries and diaries show that someone actually travelled along a certain route, industrial records may reveal the routes used to move goods, parliamentary journals and papers give details of the passage of turnpike and enclosure bills, topographies and descriptions may detail what roads were in use, and newspapers or letters may provide comment on proposals for new roads or roads in bad condition. Parish records, particularly the vestry minutes and highway surveyors' accounts, can be useful, as the parish was responsible for local road maintenance from 1555 to 1835. There are also the minutes of highway boards (usually found under Quarter Sessions proceedings), and then those of the local and county councils.

The records of the turnpike trusts themselves, plus various government returns, are of obvious interest, as are the records of tramway and bus companies. Old photographs may show roads as they were as far back as the mid-nineteenth century, and sketches and drawings go back much further. There is an endless variety of documents, and it is impossible to give a complete list. Virtually any class of document may reveal some information about roads (Stephens, 1981). A day or two spent in the local history library or record office may be very rewarding.

Maps provide an extremely valuable but surprisingly rather under-used source (Hindle, 1988). The early county maps of Saxton and Speed do not show roads, but later ones do, notably from the seventeenth century, based on Ogilby's road strip maps of 1675, and later the lists of roads in Cary's *New Itinerary* of 1798. These general topographic maps show roads as one feature among many in the landscape; in particular, the large-scale county maps of the late eighteenth century are an extremely valuable source, showing the newly-created turnpikes, as well as much of the finer detail of the road network. During the nineteenth century these maps were progressively replaced by the more detailed products of the Ordnance Survey.

In addition, there are many examples of specific road maps (those which show little else). The first are Ogilby's strip maps, but others include the Parliamentary (turnpike) Plans and other plans of proposed road changes. Virtually any type of map may depict roads: estate and tithe maps, enclosure maps and even the plans for new canals and railways may provide useful information. To help with fieldwork an old OS 6-inch map (preferably First Edition: surveyed 1841–88) is probably ideal. Vertical aerial photographs are essentially a type of map; there are various local and national collections, and they have been used to help trace Roman roads in particular.

Field evidence. Detailed library work is a necessary preliminary, but at the end of the day it is always more exciting to get out into the countryside, whether by car or on foot, to see why the Roman or turnpike surveyors chose a particular route, why a packhorse track or drove road went a particular way, or why a route has shifted its course over the years. What may be unclear from the map or the documentary record may be stunningly obvious on the ground.

Most old routes are still rights of way, and there are normally few problems of access. Unfortunately, there are quite a few landowners who regard their land as sacrosanct, even where it is crossed by a right of way; do not be put off by signs saying 'Private Land' in such a situation. It may be worthwhile consulting the definitive footpath map for an area before setting out, not only to see where you may walk legally, but also to spot some of the many long-disused roads which still survive as footpaths.

Many old routes have left physical or buried remains in the landscape which can be observed or which may have to be excavated. Roads which have been deliberately engineered, such as Roman roads or turnpikes, may have a structure which can be identified by sectioning. But those roads which came about through the continued passage of people and animals may have left nothing more than surface features such as ruts or holloways, or may have disappeared entirely from the landscape; even Roman roads can disappear after two thousand years. Another problem is that because so many roads have a long history, older surfaces have been buried beneath later ones and may have been destroyed, or made inaccessible. However, modern roads often deviate from earlier routes, and in such places the older routes may still survive, little used but still intact.

There is, however, one serious problem in field observation, namely the great difficulty of dating a road in the way one might date a house or a castle; only rarely does field or archaeological evidence provide a date. But the simple existence of a road in the landscape at a specific date is not particularly important, as it may not have been in use.

It is better (and often easier) to obtain a combination of documentary and map evidence for both the existence and the actual use of a road.

Three footnotes have to be added. First, the old (pre-1974) counties are generally used in the text, as their boundaries were the ones in use for most of the periods covered, and are still normally used in historical literature. Second, metric units are used throughout (with imperial equivalents in parenthesis), with the exception of distances which are given in miles (with kilometres in brackets). Finally, references to more detailed reading are given throughout the text; the books or articles referred to are listed in full in the Bibliography (see below pp. 153–4).

2 Early trackways

Prehistoric tracks came into use as part of the complex history of different peoples, cultures and invasions from the Stone Age through to the Iron Age. Wandering animals and the earliest peoples must have created some tracks, but it was the arrival of the Neolithic (New Stone Age) farmers around 4000 BC which seems to have led to a sudden increase in the number of settlements, and probably of trackways too. Their economy was based on farming rather than on hunting and gathering, they cleared large areas of trees for fields, and they began to trade, often over great distances.

Recent archaeological discoveries have shown that, from this date, populations generally increased fairly steadily, and the need for tracks must have grown accordingly. Indeed, this growth was helped by the climate which was warmer than today from the fourth to the second millennia BC. Stone and Bronze Age populations were clearly much larger and more sophisticated than was once thought, and trade continued to grow during this period; the items traded included agricultural goods, salt and tools. Stone axes from the central Lake District were produced from 3000 to 1500 BC – they appear to have been traded by both sea and land, and have been found throughout Britain. No doubt someone has already identified a Neolithic 'axe road', but it would be nigh on impossible to prove such an association.

The fact that these early Britons built barrows, stone circles and then henges is a measure of the complexity of their social and economic systems. The evidence is thick on the ground in such classic places as the Wiltshire Downs, but even remote wet and windy Cumbria has 12 large stone circles dating from before 1500 BC. In order to build such essentially 'useless' monuments a society requires organization, leadership, settled conditions, a surplus of food and the ability to trade. There clearly must have been an evolving network of tracks to serve the growing economic needs of those times. Life was becoming settled instead of nomadic and required definite tracks to link one place to the next, as well as to more distant places.

Finally, in the years before the Roman occupation, the British began to build hillforts; evidently the need for defence had become important, perhaps because of invasions of new settlers from the continent of Europe. Each hillfort served a large local population, which had helped or been forced to build it, and which might benefit from its protection in times of unrest. Settlements were often grouped around these hillforts and were linked to each other socially, economically and politically, as well as by physical tracks.

Beyond these local links, obvious lines of communication across the country would probably have run along the treeless ridgeways, leading so often from one hillfort to the next. This explains the concentration on ridgeways as the typical prehistoric routes, which is so apparent in the literature. By the time the Romans arrived, the ancient British tribes (by now in the Iron Age) were farming most of lowland Britain, as well as many upland areas; the distribution of their hillforts is a clear indication of the density and extent of their settlement. Trade had become very important, and the items involved included metals such as iron, tin, copper and gold, as well as food, tools and even wine.

But finding good evidence of the existence and use of tracks in this period before written history is immensely difficult. Some have been identified as surviving physical tracks, whilst others have been seen as crop marks on aerial photographs. However, it is impossible to date such tracks. Few, if any, were deliberately constructed, for like medieval roads after them, most simply came into being through the constant passage of people and animals. Despite this difficulty, topographic literature is full of unsubstantiated references to roads having prehistoric origins; no doubt many do have such a long history, but proving it is a different matter.

Nevertheless, it is very likely that many routes in use today have prehistoric origins, and this leads on to the notion that

the idea of continuity is central to a consideration of the evolution of roads. Once a 'way' became established, its general line would be used over the centuries, though its *actual* course came to vary according to the type of traffic it carried and to locally changing patterns of land occupation and ownership. (Colyer, 1984.)

This continuity only makes proving the date of origin of a track even more difficult. Virtually the only prehistoric tracks which can now be even vaguely identified as such are those which have survived because they have continued to be used, improved or

altered in later times. Some Roman improvements fossilized prehistoric routes, whereas the more recent cattle drovers tended only to destroy any evidence which still remained.

We are never likely to be able to reconstruct accurately the network of prehistoric local tracks, simply because they are unlikely to have survived intact, and even if they have, they cannot be dated. Many have probably been in use for many thousands of years, and the twentieth-century footpath sign, or layer of tarmac may well represent only the most recent act in a very long series of changes.

This lack of historical evidence has led to much speculation; perhaps the most famous is the work of Alfred Watkins (1925), who sought to find natural 'ley lines' running through the landscape, giving a network of 'old straight tracks'. Any objective study of his curious ideas reveals only random alignments and associations, and his notions of a race of Stone Age road builders are best forgotten. The very idea that Stone Age men needed sight-lines, markers and cairns to find their way about is something of an insult to them; they clearly knew their surroundings intimately. More recently, others have tried to see more complex geometric patterns and even reflections of the zodiac in the landscape. It is tempting to suggest that if you believe in any of these notions, then you may well be able to see the patterns – essentially 'they have to be believed to be seen', and that is no basis for serious scientific enquiry.

Occasionally archaeological evidence of ancient tracks does survive and the best examples have been found in the Somerset Levels, where Neolithic farmers had to build tracks across the marshy ground in order to reach the 'islands' in the marsh; the Sweet Track from the Polden Hills to Westhay is the most famous. Their construction indicates a great pressure on resources at this early period. Over forty tracks have now

1   *The West Kennett stone avenue links the ancient ritual centre of Avebury with the Ridgeway; it was probably constructed c.2000 BC, and is one of the oldest datable routeways in Britain.*

been found, the earliest, dating from about 3000 BC consists simply of bundles of twigs held in place by pegs; but by about 2000 BC there is evidence of more elaborate construction using planks or split logs (Wright, 1988).

In the monumental landscapes of Wiltshire, a deliberate creation of stone-lined avenues did take place in about 2000 BC. From Avebury, the mile-long West Kennett Avenue led to a stone circle called 'The Sanctuary', which was very close to the Great Ridgeway (Figs. 1 and 3), whilst Beckhampton Avenue led off south-westwards towards a group of round barrows. The precise purpose of such avenues is not known, though their function was probably ceremonial rather than connected with trade. However, on other parts of the Downs (and elsewhere) the physical remains of a few local prehistoric tracks have been observed, linking farms to their fields (Taylor, 1979). A complex pattern of such tracks clearly existed before the Romans arrived, but their history is often difficult to unravel, simply because the routes in use were constantly changing, and many have continued to be used, on and off, ever since.

The traditional first step in tracing prehistoric tracks in an area is to plot all the known sites that prehistoric man occupied, whether farms, monuments or forts; any surviving tracks linking such sites may well have prehistoric origins. However, this is a difficult process because our knowledge of the distribution of prehistoric sites, and of farms in particular, is very meagre.

As already noted, the best known prehistoric trackways of Britain are the ridgeways, but Taylor (1979) has thrown a good deal of doubt on their origins and importance. They achieved their status largely because they were seen to be closely related to the places where the most obvious evidence of prehistoric peoples was to be found, notably on the Wessex downlands. There is certainly no doubt that the ridges themselves are liberally scattered with prehistoric remains. It was originally thought that the valleys were then still filled with impenetrable forests, and that people would have had to use the ridgeways in order to get about. This is perhaps best summed up in Timperley and Brill's *Ancient Trackways of Wessex*, first published in 1965, which gives an exhaustive (and exhausting) description of every possible ridge route in Wessex. In 32 chapters, there are over a dozen named ridgeways plus their numerous branches, as well as various other ways and tracks (Fig. 2).

The argument now levelled against the ridgeways being important prehistoric routes is that the distribution of prehistoric sites and finds as known today does not reveal a particular clustering along many of these ridges. It appears that earlier researchers may have fallen into the trap of basing their ideas on very limited data. The first prehistoric sites to be noted were the obvious remains on the ridges and downlands, but more recent work has shown that most prehistoric settlements were actually in the valleys, on what must have been better land even in those days. In Northamptonshire, Taylor demonstrates

2   *The Wessex Ridgeways. Many routes have been identified, often with little evidence for their prehistoric use. (After Timperley and Brill, 1983)*

that the so-called 'Jurassic Way', which was first proposed in 1940 as running along the Jurassic limestone ridge, simply does not act as a route connecting the numerous prehistoric sites which were known forty years later. He makes a very convincing case for this route being a twentieth-century invention.

This is perhaps a rather special case, and it is not so easy to make out a similar case

disproving the more prominent chalk ridgeways further south. However, Taylor goes on to show that even the Icknield Way, which is undoubtedly a prehistoric route, is also not particularly well related to the known prehistoric sites, and his conclusion is that none of the ridgeways was particularly important as a prehistoric route.

It can, however, be argued that this evidence is largely irrelevant. If a suggested prehistoric route is not closely related to the archaeological sites, then perhaps this may be simply because the two are largely independent of each other. The factors which must have influenced the location of farms, forts or burial sites are not the same as those which controlled the direction of travel and thus the creation of routes. The ancient Britons surely preferred to live where there was good quality well-watered land. But their criteria for choosing a route would certainly have been very different: a route had to go in the appropriate direction, and it ought to be easy and safe to traverse. In these respects the ridgeways may or may not have been suitable.

Thus the fact that known prehistoric sites do not cluster along a route is not a particularly good argument that the route was not then in use; more detailed local examination is needed in each particular case. A much better argument against the use of the ridgeways is their lack of water for animals. Many of these old routes were certainly in use before the Romans arrived, but precisely when they came into use, and how important they actually were, will probably remain an insoluble mystery. Overall, the balance of the argument is probably in favour of their prehistoric origins, and they may be the first 'highways' in more ways than one.

Several of the ridgeways are described here; the best examples are those which traverse the downlands of southern England. But it is important to realize that originally they must have looked very different from the way they appear today. They were certainly less pronounced and much wider, as they were only rarely constrained by other features in the landscape. By contrast, modern tracks are usually walled or hedged in, and even today's tracks across open hillsides are probably much narrower and more obvious than their prehistoric counterparts. Further, it has long been suggested that most had

'summer ways' which ran along lower routes, used in dry weather when there was no water on the top of the ridge. Whether these summer ways are prehistoric in origin is impossible to determine, they are just as likely to date from medieval and later times when these routes were used for the droving of large numbers of cattle.

This suggestion of duplicated ways may, however, be based on a limited study of the modern landscape. It is much more likely that, until the downs were enclosed in the last 200 years, all the ridge routes were simply much broader than at present as there were no walls, fences or hedges to constrict the routes. Thus they were probably not the simple single or duplicated tracks and lanes which appear on maps today, but were much broader lines of travel, perhaps a mile or two wide, along which each traveller, trader or drover chose the best route available.

The Great Ridgeway and the Icknield Way

This immense route stretches across England from the south coast near Axminster to the Wash (Wright, 1988). Perhaps its most famous section is that crossing the Marlborough Downs east of Avebury (Fig. 3). One guidebook describes this section as:

a distinct and unmistakable track, seldom hindered by overgrowth or obstruction, swinging along mile after mile between widely spaced fences or hedges. (Jennett, 1976.)

Overton Hill now marks the start of a modern long-distance footpath along or close to this ancient route. Until this new footpath was created in 1973, many parts of the old track were derelict, or used only as farm tracks. Thus after a long period of neglect, the Ridgeway has re-emerged in its new guise as a long-distance footpath.

3 *Ancient routeways near Avebury.
The modern Ridgeway Path
represents what was formerly a much
wider route; the West Kennett Avenue,
a Roman road and a Saxon herepath
can also be seen.*

4 *The Ridgeway path running westwards from the hillfort at Uffington; the modern enclosed path is some distance from the edge of the downs, the scarp overlooking the Vale of White Horse is half a mile to the right.*

For the first few miles north of Overton Hill, the route crosses what is a landscape with many visible ancient features – a glance at the map or at the landscape itself shows Silbury Hill and the Avebury stone circle and avenue only a mile to the west. In addition there are numerous tumuli, ditches, standing stones, circles, earthworks, field systems and barrows; amidst all of this (and largely ignoring it all) the present Great Ridgeway path climbs straight up on to the downs towards Hackpen Hill. There are indications of other old roads here: a Roman road and the Wiltshire Herepath (a Saxon 'army road') both cross the Ridgeway within a couple of miles. The fact that the herepath heads straight for Avebury suggests that it too has prehistoric origins.

After 5½ miles (9km) the route passes close to Barbury Castle, the first of many hillforts along the way. The present ridgeway path does not actually pass through any of these forts, but as we have already seen, the prehistoric route was probably much wider than today's enclosed track, and thus the old route was well able to serve the forts if needed. The forts were deliberately situated on the top of the scarp, whilst the present ridgeway is rarely on the ridge, keeping just below the skyline (Fig. 4). The idea that the ancient Britons wanted to keep out of sight is pure conjecture; the present confined route between the hedges was probably only fixed within the last 200 years, when the farmers, enclosing their fields, left a narrow track for the drovers who still passed by (Fig. 5).

Just before Barbury Castle, the line of the Great Ridgeway as shown on OS maps descends from the ridge for several miles, whilst the modern Ridgeway Path goes straight through the castle, keeping to the ridge. At one point the two routes are almost 4 miles (6km) apart; this modern bifurcation no doubt mirrors the situation in prehistoric times. Twelve miles (20km) further on, in the Vale of White Horse below Uffington Castle, the twentieth-century metalled equivalent of this old route is the B4507, but it runs along the foot of the scarp; both roads were clearly still in use when Rocque drew his county map in 1761 (Fig. 6).

Going eastwards, the name Icknield Way first appears on maps as a road below the main route of the Great Ridgeway to the north of Lambourn Downs. However, north-east of the Thames crossing at Goring gap, this name is adopted by the various parallel routes running along the northern edge of the Chilterns. Here it is very clear that the Way was originally a mile wide.

The Icknield Way certainly did not begin life as the road or bridlepath or green lane we now see . . . Icknield was then . . . an intertwining of many paths . . . (Crosher, 1973.)

Eventually these have been confined into the two, three or four parallel tracks visible today; some are still routes, whether roads, tracks or paths, whilst others only survive as hedges or boundaries.

Icknield Way is essentially a continuation of the Great Ridgeway, but there are two

---

5 *A typical view of the Ridgeway long-distance path near Wantage, now enclosed by hedges.*

---

6 *Rocque's map of Berkshire (1761) shows 'The Ridge Way' on the downs above the Vale of White Horse. (Reproduced by courtesy of H. Margary.)*

7 *A long-distance footpath sign, confusingly seen on the Icknield Way.*

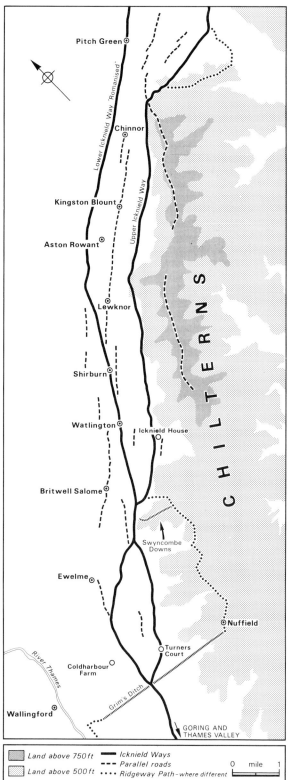

important differences: the first is that most of the tracks are at the foot of the scarp – and it is odd that this section of the long-distance path is still referred to as the Ridgeway (Fig. 7). The second difference is that the Romans improved many lengths of one of the old tracks, essentially making it into a Roman road. Many later documentary references are to Icknield *Street*, a word which often denotes a Roman road. It is dealt with in this chapter as the origins of the route as a whole are clearly pre-Roman.

Starting from Goring, the first 9½ miles (15km) were not improved by the Romans and the modern Ridgeway footpath takes an entirely different route until reaching the foot of Swyncombe Downs, having covered some 12 miles (20km) to reach the same point. The Way passes through a gap in Grim's Ditch, one of many prehistoric earthworks built across the ridgeways, and immediately there are a number of parallel tracks which are the sole remnants of this former wide routeway (Figs. 8 and 9).

The Romanized route is described in great

8 *Surviving lines of the former mile-wide Icknield Way beneath the Chilterns; one line was Romanized, and another is now the long-distance Ridgeway Path, though the latter takes an entirely new route in places.*

9 *One of the remnants of the former mile-wide Icknield Way running beneath the Chiltern scarp near Lewknor; it is crossed at this point by the M40, thus one of Britain's newest roads crosses one of the oldest.*

detail by the Viatores (1964). A possible sign of Roman work is a straight alignment from Turners Court to Lewknor, but the first good evidence is the alignment of the B4009, running north-west from Watlington to within a mile of Lewknor. The Roman road is then lost until it reappears north of Lewknor on a new alignment; here it is seen as a track or path parallel to the modern B road for 3 miles (5km), until it is joined by that road at Chinnor (Fig. 10). In this length there are still three parallel tracks: the northernmost is the Romanized Lower Icknield Way; the middle is the modern B road, the sole remnant of the old wide route still surviving as a through road; whilst the southernmost track is now called the Upper Icknield Way, and is followed here by the modern long-distance path. None of the routes runs along the ridge of the Chilterns at this point,

10 *The Romanized Icknield Way now changes from a field track to a metalled road on entering the village of Chinnor.*

though it has been suggested that there may well have been such a route. The routes which survive are clearly very different from the ridgeways of Wessex.

This duplication of routes continues along much of the line of the Icknield Way. The modern Ridgeway footpath ends at Beacon Hill, near Ivinghoe, whilst the Romanized Icknield Way continues through Tring, Dunstable (where it crosses Watling Street), Luton, Letchworth, Baldock and Royston, to a junction north of the Roman town of Great Chesterford. It then continues by way of Newmarket and Thetford to the Wash, its final section lying parallel to the later Roman Peddars Way. Why the Romans should have improved the trackway, and also built a new route alongside for almost 40 miles (64km) is a mystery; it certainly shows that having good routes to the Wash was important to them.

The Icknield Way is one of the most complicated of all routes in Britain – virtually any route roughly parallel to the ridge may well be a remnant of the old mile-wide way along which people used to travel. Some of the surviving routes of the Icknield Way have been straightened by the enclosure surveyors (see Chapter 9), others have main roads running along them (for example the A505 from Baldock to Royston, and the A11 from Great Chesterford to Newmarket), whilst others are simply green lanes or footpaths, or have gone out of use altogether. The modern long-distance footpath is just as much a part of all this history as any other, even though, as a through route, it was created only in 1973.

Other prehistoric tracks

Of the many trackways identified in Wessex, the Harrow Way is one of the more important, as it led eastwards from the Stonehenge area to join the what later

became known as the Pilgrims' Way which runs along the North Downs to the east coast of Kent (see Chapter 4). This road competes with the main Ridgeway for the title of the oldest road in Britain; its name probably means 'hard way', referring to the chalk underfoot (Timperley & Brill, 1983). From Farnham, two routes have been identified (main and summer ways?) which joined beyond Basingstoke; the track then passed just to the north of Andover and is followed closely by the modern A303 to Amesbury and Stonehenge (Wright, 1988). It may well have crossed the Ridgeway close to the place where the A350 crosses the A303, between Warminster and Shaftesbury, before going on further west (see Fig. 2).

As noted above, all the possible prehistoric tracks are difficult to authenticate, and outside southern England only a handful have a demonstrable claim to antiquity. There certainly were many prehistoric tracks in the north and west of Britain, but perhaps they had less traffic, were less prominent in the landscape and have survived less well than those tracks on the chalk downlands. The problem with such routes is that there has been a tendency to assume that any track running across isolated high ridges and passing the odd tumulus must automatically have prehistoric origins, just as had been assumed (with rather more certainty) in southern England. Although definite proof is almost inevitably missing, several deserve a brief mention.

The Exmoor Ridgeway, which runs across the moor north of the B3223 and B3358, has been tentatively identified as a Bronze Age trackway, apparently also known to and used by the Saxons. Perhaps similar in date is the Kerry Hills Ridgeway which leads into the much later town of Bishop's Castle in the mid-Welsh borders; it has been described as the oldest road in Wales. It was certainly important in the days of the drovers, when it was one of the main routes into England (see Chapter 6). It is associated with several other high-level routes, including the Clun–Clee Ridgeway and the 'Portway' along the top of the Long Mynd (Portway is a Saxon word for an important road leading to a market or port). Walks along both these ridgeway routes are described in Dunn (1986), and part of the Exmoor route is outlined in Toulson (1983). Several Bronze Age tracks on Dartmoor are also suggested in Toulson (1984), though with such routes she does tend to get involved in ley lines.

In Derbyshire, several routes between the major monuments have been tentatively identified, including a route from the hillfort on Mam Tor, running to the south past three other forts. It is known as the Old Portway, and its origins may well be contemporary with the use of the forts. It has, of course, been much altered subsequently, notably during its later history as a packhorse route (Dodd, 1980).

Into this well populated land with its network of tracks came the Romans, who were to impose a new and largely independent system of engineered roads. The old main tracks which had served the British for so long generally went in directions of little use to the Romans. They were also clearly physically inadequate for the new military and trading needs and many must have gone out of use. However, the local tracks from one farmstead to the next must have continued to be used, and many have no doubt remained in use ever since.

3 Roman roads

The Roman invasion of Britain in AD 43 is one of the most important turning points in British history; not only did it herald almost four hundred years of Roman rule, but the Romans were also to leave a legacy of forts, towns and roads which have influenced the urban structure, road system and landscape to this day. Indeed, many British towns and roads have been built on top of or alongside their Roman predecessors. By AD 47 the Romans had advanced as far as a line from Exeter to Lincoln, and the remarkably straight Foss Way was built as a strategic road to serve the Roman legions. It took the Romans over 45 years to bring the rest of England and Wales firmly under their control, though this was finally achieved by Agricola who conquered Wales and northern England in the years around AD 80. The attempt to conquer Scotland was unsuccessful, and after several forays, the border was established along Hadrian's Wall. It was begun in the 120s, and became the permanent frontier from 163.

In studying Roman roads it is not possible to agree with Margary (1973) that 'the roads were laid out as a carefully planned system'. On the contrary, there was much piecemeal development, with each road being built for a specific purpose at a particular date; two or three adjacent roads might have been laid out in conjunction with each other, but clearly there was no overall master plan. In order to have undertaken such a plan the Romans would have needed a detailed map of much of Britain; there is no evidence that such a map ever existed. Having said that, it is evident that each individual road was carefully planned and laid out with knowledge of and respect for the country through which it was to pass.

Many of the early roads were clearly military in nature, linking one fort to the next, either to allow the rapid and easy movement of troops and provisions, or to subdue, conquer and then control the country. This is especially true of roads in Wales and the north of England, areas which were controlled by the military for many years. These military roads were imposed on the landscape, and they took little account of what was there already, except on the rare occasions when they improved existing tracks. When conditions became more settled and trade increased in importance, many of the major trading routes must have been between the existing forts and towns, and thus along the roads which had already been built.

Some later roads were built primarily for trade, especially in the south-eastern part of the country, which was soon under civil rather than military control. Johnston (1979) argues that there is a clear distinction

11 *The network of main Roman roads; many lengths are uncertain or missing. (After Margary, 1973.)*

between the planned military roads, and those which grew by 'natural growth'. But there are mysteries too. Some obvious links were never built, and Roman towns failed to grow at many major junctions, such as Old Sarum and Badbury Rings.

The total length of Roman roads will probably never be known. One reason for this is that new sections are continually being found; another is that there was a hierarchy of roads, built to different standards and widths. The main roads were the well-built highways funded by the military or the state, next in the scale came the local roads financed by each district, and then the private roads serving individual estates, farms or villas, or dividing up agricultural land for new settlement. The major Roman roads vary greatly in their importance and in their levels of engineering; however, there is no simple relationship between the two. Only the more important roads are likely to survive and be traceable; thus we can only reconstruct the network of main roads with any degree of certainty (Fig. 11). This network probably totalled close to 10,000 miles (16,000km).

The minor road system has generally been forgotten or ignored, largely because of the immense difficulty of seeing it. Hoskins (1955) said that

We have been bemused too long by the great military roads of the Romans and have not given enough thought and research to the local 'economic' roads . . .

and Hooke (1977) has commented that

the network of [main] Roman roads thrown across the West Midland countryside . . . was obviously inadequate to serve the needs of such a region.

There must have been a great mileage of local tracks between settlements and fields, which had very little (if any) engineering or surfacing; many were no doubt pre-Roman in origin. It may be possible to distinguish them from the main Roman roads by the terms used in Anglo-Saxon and later charters – Roman roads are usually termed *straets*, whilst the minor tracks are *paeths* or *wegs*.

There is no way of estimating the mileage of the minor roads and tracks, but many lanes and farm tracks must have been in use in Roman times, even though they may now not look in the least like what we think of as 'typical' Roman roads. Occasionally some evidence of these local tracks remains, even if only on aerial photographs where they can be seen perhaps leading to a Roman villa, fields or some other site. Taylor (1979) gives examples of minor Roman roads in Dorset; three tracks near Maiden Newton can be seen to link several Roman fields and farmsteads, whilst near Milton Abbas four tracks lead out from a Roman village, two surviving as embanked holloways and one as a terraceway.

The Romans applied their love of straight lines to the laying out of fields and field roads. The process by which land was divided up by surveyors is called 'centuriation', as it was based multiples of a hundred. The basic unit of length was the *actus* of 120 Roman feet (116 statute feet; 35m), and plot dimensions were made up of various multiples of it. Margary (1948) demonstrated the evidence for such deliberate planning near the village of Ripe, east of Lewes (Fig. 12). At first sight, such patterns might appear to be those of Parliamentary enclosure (see Chapter 9), but there was no such enclosure here, and the layout is in fact much older. These lanes, with their striking rectangular pattern, are essentially the 'occupation roads' of Roman times. However, the pattern has strayed somewhat from the original, just as one might expect after almost 2000 years; such changes have not occurred in the 200 years since enclosure (Fig. 13). Centuriation has been noted elsewhere, including Rochester,

12 and 13 *The surviving network of Roman roads and fields around Ripe in Sussex. The pattern of centuriation is shown both by a recent map, and by Gardner and Gream's map of the county (1795) (left). (Reproduced by courtesy of H. Margary.)*

as well as at such unlikely spots as east Manchester and around Penrith.

Most of the field evidence of minor Roman roads no longer exists; few of these tracks were engineered or surfaced and they may well have been ploughed out, or have been in use ever since. In such cases any Roman origins are impossible to see or prove and the vast majority of such lesser features of the Roman landscape have long since disappeared. The ploughing up of the downlands of southern England during the Second World War certainly destroyed many examples of these tracks. Of necessity, therefore, this chapter concentrates on the major routes.

The more important Roman roads vary a good deal in their present appearance,

not least because of differences in their construction. Typically they have an agger (the raised central ridge), usually bounded by ditches on either side. Local materials were used in construction, whether beach pebbles, gravel or quarried rock. Their width varies a good deal; the agger may be between 3 and 8m (10 and 25ft) across, and the ditches may be 5 to 26m (15 to 85ft) apart. However, the agger of a major road such as Ermine Street can be up to 15m (50ft) wide, and 1.5m (5ft) in height. These roads vary quite considerably along their length. They are embanked in some places and not in others, and they may not be metalled throughout. These inconsistencies seem to have been the result of both different engineers building different sections, as well as the different requirements for each part of the route. The less engineered sections of a road may now be much less obvious in the landscape. Many of the Roman mountain roads were evidently not metalled, and only seem to have received any attention from the engineers when the need for their use arose. Such roads are often little more than terraces cut into hillsides, and can be particularly difficult to trace today.

It is of course a well-known fact (at least according to Sellar and Yeatman's *1066 and All That*) that 'the Roman roads ran absolutely straight in all directions and all led to Rome'! This glorious oversimplification is not totally removed from the truth; Roman roads were *direct* rather than straight, and usually proceeded in a series of short straight alignments, sometimes aiming from a great distance directly for their goal, but often diverting in order to avoid boggy ground, awkward river crossings, or some other difficulty. When confronted by a steep hill, they either embarked on a set of zigzags, took a more circuitous route, or simply went straight up the slope; these roads were principally designed for the rapid movement of men, horses and pack animals, rather than for the passage of laden carts.

The use of straight alignments was fundamentally a matter of simplicity and convenience for the surveyors and engineers; yet they chose their routes with great skill, taking care to use the natural routes through the landscape wherever possible. The surveyors clearly undertook a general survey of the whole route first, looking for the best lines. It is simply not known how the long alignments were made; the Foss Way runs for over 200 miles (322km), yet is never more than 8 miles (13km) from the direct line between Axminster and Lincoln. The detached alignments of Stane Street form a rather different, but equally good example (see p.36 and Fig. 16). Changes of alignment were often made on high ground, so that the next section of road could more easily be

laid out. There is a great contrast between the long straight lengths such as those taken by Watling Street across the Midlands (now the A5), and the much more pragmatic design of Roman roads through the mountainous areas of Wales or the Lake District; yet even here, the roads always tend to proceed in short straight stretches wherever possible.

Not all straight roads are of Roman origin; many more were created by Parliamentary enclosure in the years around 1800, but these are usually obvious both in the landscape and in the written record, and they never connect one Roman site with another (see Chapter 9). The rare exception to this is when a Roman road was made part of an enclosure road system (see Fig. 28).

Tracing Roman roads

There is still great scope for the Roman road hunter, whether amateur or professional, as many roads have yet to be fully traced. It has to be said, though, that most of the 'easy' Roman roads have already been found. The standard technique involves historical and cartographic research followed by field observation, backed up by proper excavation only if necessary (Bagshawe, 1979). There is one piece of contemporary written evidence for Roman roads, namely the *Antonine Itinerary*, which is a list of the main roads of the empire – 15 routes are given in Britain, most of which have now been traced on the ground.

The first step in any research is to obtain a description and map of known Roman roads; Margary (1973) is the basic starting point, but he deals only with the most important roads and is now rather out of date. So the next step is to check in local libraries to see what recent research has been done. There may well be a local archaeological society or journal, and there is usually also a 'Roman road expert' in each area who will be quite well known. The Archaeology Branch of the Ordnance Survey also keeps detailed records, as do various local archaeological units. All this research will reveal many gaps in the known network.

Several areas have already received detailed treatment, including the Weald by Margary himself (1948), and the south-east Midlands by a group of his enthusiastic followers (Viatores, 1964; see p.38), but much remains to be done. The present author was amazed to find, in researching the Roman roads of the Lake District (1984), that no one had previously tried to reconstruct the network in that well-known and much written-about corner of Britain.

In order to understand the Roman road system in an area, it is important to determine when each fort and town was established, as the main roads to each place would have been built at the same time as the settlements, if not before. Indeed, in the early stages of the military occupation it would have been normal practice to build the main penetrative roads first, to back up the invasion, with troops living in temporary camps. Some forts were evidently built as afterthoughts, placed on roads at an appropriate place for victualling, usually a day's march apart (about 10−15 miles or 16−24km). On the other hand, many forts later went out of use, and the roads to them decayed or were replaced.

Next, maps should be consulted; virtually any old map of an area may be of use. Eighteenth-century county maps and early editions of the Ordnance Survey one-inch map are good starting points for getting a general view of a route, but detailed work requires old 6-inch OS maps. These maps were first surveyed in the second half of the nineteenth century and they show field and parish boundaries and place-names in considerable detail. They also show roads before recent alterations, as well as features no longer evident in the landscape, for

example those which have been built over or destroyed by ploughing. Furthermore they may be freely copied if over 50 years old. Aerial photographs, if available, may also be of great use.

The importance of parish boundaries in tracing Roman roads may not be immediately obvious. Most seem to have been created after the Romans had left, in the long and often unsettled period known as the Dark Ages. When people were choosing sites for their farms or hamlets, they clearly avoided the Roman roads, probably to keep out of the way of any marauders; the aggers of the roads would also form an obvious boundary line. Consequently, throughout large areas of England, parish boundaries follow Roman roads. Watling Street (A5) has virtually no early settlements on it, and is a parish boundary for most of its length. This general rule can be used to help trace missing sections of road. However, a straight road with a parish boundary running along it is not automatically Roman; features which are specifically Roman must be sought as confirmation.

The next step is to note any obvious Roman detail, whether known roads, milestones, towns, forts, burials or villas, and to add the various place-names (and field names) which are associated with Roman sites and roads. Roman road names include Street (also Stretton, Stratford), Gate (meaning road), Coldharbour and Caldecot, and perhaps Ford, Stone, Stane (referring to the metalling), as well as any Ridges, Ridgeways or Causeways. Most of these are self-explanatory but Coldharbour and Caldecot are not; these place-names are commonly found close to Roman roads and probably had their origins in referring to roadside shelters.

With the aid of a ruler, extending whatever short alignments have been found, it is often possible to see much longer alignments of roads, hedges, paths or

14 *The dual carriageway of the A419 north of Swindon is directly on top of the Roman road from Silchester to Cirencester. The road has probably been a landscape feature for almost two thousand years.*

boundaries at this stage. The search is simply for a series of short straight alignments connecting one Roman site to another.

If a new alignment is found, then it is time to get into the field to see if there are any remains on the ground; indeed the main evidence for the Roman road system has always lain in the landscape itself. This can be the most exciting part of the process, for the options open to the Roman surveyor should start to become clearer – features which cannot be shown on the map (such as minor steep slopes, marshy ground or former marshy ground) can be seen at first hand. A good imagination is needed to try

to envisage what the countryside may have been like two thousand years ago. Of course, many Roman roads are still in use, and the original engineering may now lie beneath tarmac (Fig. 14). Some roads may have been obscured by centuries of erosion, traffic or soil movement, removed by ploughing or tree planting, whilst others may now simply be inaccessible due to unhelpful landowners. It is surprising, though, how many Roman roads are still rights of way.

The final proof of Roman date may require a section to be dug, but professional help *must* be sought as digging is destructive and a bad excavation may destroy valuable

15 *Rocque's map of Surrey (1768) shows Stane Street clearly where it passes through Ockley; this short section is now the A29. To the north, the road disappears, but there are two 'Cole Harbour' place-names at the top of the extract. (Reproduced by courtesy of H. Margary.)*

16 *The alignments of Stane Street between London and Chichester display the great accuracy of Roman road surveying over long distances.*

evidence. In any case modern archaeology tends to regard digging as the last resort, only undertaken when historical and geographical research has failed. There will always be lengths where there is no physical evidence, and obtaining absolute proof of a Roman road for any great length is very difficult; a string of detached observations will often be the best that can be obtained.

There are so many Roman roads that it is clearly impossible to mention more than a few here. This is a rather arbitrary selection, but they are chosen to illustrate the different types of road, the different features which they exhibit and the problems involved in tracing them.

Stane Street

Stane Street is probably the best known Roman road south of London, it connects that city to Chichester, then the tribal capital of Sussex. Its name refers to its stony surface, and it is first referred to as 'Stanstret' in 1270; it is clearly shown on Rocque's map of Surrey (1768) (Fig. 15). It was the subject of a very readable but rather inaccurate book by Hilaire Belloc (1913). The route is described in detail by Margary (1948); much of it remains in use. The route has only nine alignments, of which three can be described as major. The first alignment from London heads directly for Chichester's east gate, which is 56 miles (90km) distant and obviously out of sight; it maintains this line as far as Ewell. Further south a 12 mile (20km) section points directly back towards London (Fig. 16). How these detached but precisely surveyed alignments were laid out remains a mystery.

On the ground, however, the road frequently deviates from the precise line in response to local topography:

such modifications of a major alignment occur very frequently . . . and a slavish adherence to a rigid line is certainly not to be looked for if the ground does not favour it. (Margary, 1948.)

From London the road leaves the first alignment at Ewell in order to take advantage of travelling on the chalk for an extra 3 miles (5km). The road passes through the Mole Gap at Dorking, and leaves the precise alignment for a mile; here it

changes abruptly to a terrace around the head of the combe . . . Even in this sinuous course the famous Roman straightness is not forgotten . . . [it is] 'a flexible line of straight pieces'. (Johnston, 1979.)

Nearer Chichester, it leaves the alignment again, this time for almost 2 miles (3km) at Bignor Hill; it was built as a terraceway to tackle the hill, and deviates by up to 365m (1200ft) from the direct line. Margary also demonstrates that the course then shown on the Ordnance Survey maps is incorrect in places. At Oakwood Hill, north-west of Horsham, the OS map assumed that the road went straight down a steep bank and across a stream. In fact the correct line involved a diversion to cross 180m (600ft) upstream; this line is followed by the parish boundary (Fig. 17a and b).

Rochester to Hastings

Margary (1948) also describes a very different group of roads in the Kentish Weald, south of the section of Watling Street between Rochester and Canterbury. Although so close to London, this was a remote and difficult area in Roman times, only thinly populated. Margary points out that although these roads are

distinctly Roman in parts of their layout and construction, they are yet very imperfect in the accuracy of the alignments . . . a circumstance which suggests a relatively late date for their construction . . .

17a and b *Two examples of the way in which Roman road builders adapted the direct line of Stane Street to meet local conditions. (After Margary, 1948.)*

The main road was probably built for commercial rather than military reasons, in particular to serve the Wealden iron industry in the area around Battle. At its southern end the road probably led to long silted-up ports, such as at Bodiam (now east Sussex).

Some parts of the route are now overlain by modern roads, notably the A229, through Staplehurst to Sissinghurst, but elsewhere the route can be traced by aggers, holloways, cuttings, zigzags or merely as hedgerows along the line of the road. Only rarely is it followed by parish boundaries, suggesting that it ceased to be an important feature in the landscape after the Romans left. In several places Margary again found that the old OS alignments were wrong. A peculiarity of the roads in this area is their use of iron slag as road metalling.

Watling Street

There are numerous roads now called Watling Street, the most important of which led from Dover through Canterbury, London, St Albans, Dunstable and Towcester to meet the Foss Way at High Cross. It was later continued to the Welsh border at Wroxeter from where another road (the 'Western Watling Street') linked Caerleon and Chester. It is probably the best known Roman road in Britain. It remained important even in the 'Dark Ages' when much of it formed the boundary between the English and Danish Mercian kingdoms. Most of it is still in use, notably as the A2 and A5, and thus much of the Roman engineering has been destroyed. Occasionally, though, the modern road is not always directly on top its Roman precursor.

The section from London to Towcester is given by three routes in the *Antonine Itinerary*, and it is described in great detail by the Viatores (1964). Edgware Road marks its course out of London, and only two main alignments were needed to cover the 19 miles (30km) to the important town of Verulamium, just west of the later St Albans. The route is now largely overlain by the A5, including the dog-leg at Elstree, yet the agger is still visible in a few places, despite the continuing use of the road and the great number of buildings constructed alongside.

Because so much of this road has remained in continuous service as one of the chief thoroughfares of England, and now carries an immensely heavy traffic, its form has been greatly modified for long distances, first by turnpike works in the coaching era, and more recently by large-scale widenings. There is thus little chance of seeing any relics of its original state, and all that can be observed now is the layout of the alignments and they way in which parish and county boundaries frequently follow it. (Margary, 1973.)

Nevertheless, the route is easily followed by car, and the rare occasions where the old route still survives can easily be found and visited.

Beyond Verulamium, the road had to find an easy route across the Chilterns, and in two places the original line and the A5 part company. These are from Friar's Wash to Markyate (north of Flamstead), and again from Markyate to the outskirts of Dunstable, where it crosses the Romanized Icknield Way (see Chapter 2). North of Dunstable, the Roman road took a gentle zigzag to cross the final chalk ridge at Puddlehill, with gradients of up to 1 in 8; a short section of the Roman summit cutting still survives (Viatores, 1964).

Dorchester to Alconbury

The Viatores (1964) concentrated their efforts on the area bounded by London, Silchester, High Cross and Godmanchester. They were able to give immense detail about the main roads, and even corrected portions of roads which were well known and might have been expected to have been well established by the time they wrote. Their work has been criticized for the inclusion of roads of doubtful Roman origin; nevertheless, they described an extensive radial system of roads from Verulamium, plus several long distance routes. In addition they revealed some of the elusive local roads and these are much more difficult to trace and prove as Roman; they were never as well engineered, and were less likely to have had long alignments. Of the 49 roads in their survey (totalling 850 miles (1370km)) only 11 were known previously.

Their major single discovery was a 65 mile (105km) long road running north–east from Dorchester to Ermine Street, which had almost entirely disappeared from the landscape; its discovery began by the checking of a single place-name (Causeway End at Wootton, Bedford). The route is remarkably direct, and it lies parallel to, and between, the Foss Way and Icknield Way, but, unlike them, it has numerous changes of alignment and diversions. It does, though, have the classic feature of being made up of straight stretches with changes of alignment on higher ground. Other evidence included medieval road names, place-names, a paved ford, plus various Roman sites and finds. It is obviously no longer a through route, but many minor roads still use it for short stretches. There are several good surviving sections of agger (though rarely more than 6m (20ft) wide), but often it is represented by nothing more than hedges, parish boundaries, or as a footpath or holloway. There was a settlement where it crosses Akeman Street.

It crosses Watling Street at Little Brickhill, and ends at Alconbury where it joins Ermine Street. This was clearly one of the later cross-country routes built for economic reasons.

Foss Way (Fosse Way)

This road was constructed by about AD 47, and it used to be thought that it was the north-west frontier of Roman Britain at that time, partly due to its (later) name, meaning 'ditch road'. However, there were several forts in front of that line, and it is perhaps best seen as a strategic road, allowing rearward communication between the various legions. A curious feature is that its surveyed line is virtually parallel to two sections of Stane Street, over 85 miles (135km) away (Jones and Mattingly, 1990). Most of the Foss Way is still visible in the landscape, whether as a modern road or lane, or just as a path or hedgerow. It runs for 208 miles (335km) from Axmouth via Axminster, Ilchester, Bath, Cirencester, Moreton-in-Marsh, High Cross, Leicester and Newark to Lincoln, always within a few miles of the overall alignment; this remarkable directness is a testament to Roman surveying.

It is no longer a through route, though modern major roads follow it for some length, for example from south of Ilchester to Bath (A303, A37, A367), from south of Cirencester to Halford (A429), and finally for 58 miles (93km) from just south of Leicester to Lincoln (A46). But most of these modern major roads are going across the line of the Foss Way, and only follow it where it suits them. An interesting section lies immediately to the south of the A5 at High Cross, where it is now a minor road (with a couple of miles as a B road) for over 27 miles (43km) towards Stow-on-the-Wold. It is clearly signposted as the 'Fosse Way', its lack of traffic in sharp contrast to

18 *An unclassified modern road along the line of the Foss(e) Way, just south of its junction with Watling Street (A5) at High Cross.*

the busy A5 (Fig. 18). A walk along one of the sections which survives only as a path, south-west of Cirencester, is described by Dunn (1986).

Welsh roads and the Sarn Helen

The Romans took a long time to complete their conquest of Wales, and the road system must have emerged over quite an extended period. The 'Western Watling Street' along the border is certainly earlier in date than the roads connected with the invasion of Anglesey in AD 60, or the general conquest of Wales in the mid 70s. Wales had a long period of military control, and there is thus a dense scattering of some three dozen forts. The detailed chronology of these forts has been worked out; most were occupied only during the early stages of conquest and pacification. After about AD 125 only a few forts continued to be occupied (Jones and Mattingly, 1990). Thus the road network expanded and contracted in response to these changing needs; many roads were in use for only a few decades.

The Roman road system in Wales is still imperfectly known, chiefly through lack of investigation. However, it can be more difficult to trace roads through hilly areas as the roads were narrower than in the lowlands, have few long alignments and both surfacing and good aggers are rare. The area with the best developed road system is in South Wales, designed to subdue the tribe of the Silures – for example, roads fan out in six directions from the fort at Brecon. But elsewhere in Wales there were few Roman roads, though these were evidently planned with great care to encircle the central hills. There were legionary fortresses along the border at Chester, Wroxeter, Usk and Caerleon, and a rectangle of roads linked that border with Brecon and Carmarthen in the south and with Caernarfon in the north. The road running down the western edge of this rectangle is known as the Sarn Helen (Colyer, 1984) (Fig. 19).

The road's name probably means 'Road of the Legion' (*Sarn-y-Lleng*), though other more romantic explanations have been suggested. In fact, the name Sarn Helen is applied to many vaguely Roman looking roads throughout Wales. The route of *the* Sarn Helen is still uncertain in many places, notably in the middle part of its course. It starts in the Conwy valley (rather than at Caernarfon), and one of the first clear sections is near Ffestiniog, where it is seen as a 3m (9ft) wide track north of the Ffestiniog to Bala road. South of Ffestiniog the Roman road is not overlain by the A487, but lies a little to the east, first as a lane and then as a terrace on the hillside.

Of the central section from Pennal to Lledrod, Margary (1973) said:

If there have been doubtful portions of Sarn Helen already described it should be said at once that this section of it is still extremely

19 *The Sarn Helen (from Pennal to Llanio) and associated roads in west Wales. (After Colyer, 1984.)*

uncertain . . . and it can only warrant inclusion here because it is virtually certain that there must have been a through road . . .

The whole of the route south of Pennal is dealt with in great detail by Colyer (1984),

20 *High Street and the Kirkstone Pass Roman roads; High Street may have been little more than a temporary route, soon replaced by a lower and easier route through the fells.*

though he clearly points out that there is still no definite proof that the roads he describes are Roman:

This part of Cardiganshire is criss-crossed by scores, if not hundreds of miles of trackways of uncertain vintage, and it is hardly surprising that other courses for *Sarn Helen* have been postulated.

Very few roads here have been excavated.

Writing later than Margary, and with much more detailed local knowledge, Colyer was able to incorporate the recent discoveries of forts which the roads served. The most important of these were the fortlet at Erglodd and the large fort at Penllwyn (3 miles (5km) from Aberystwyth, overlooking the river Rheidol) both discovered only in 1970s. These discoveries fixed two more places through which the road must have run. The next fort is at Trawsgoed on the river Ystwyth; Colyer suggests a route further inland than did Margary, one which climbs to join the A485 south of Bronnant, where there was yet another fort. Margary had thought that the present main road from Lledrod was the likely route. The A road coincides with the Roman line for 1½ miles (2km), and then the B4578 takes over, leading directly to the next fort at Llanio. Throughout this difficult area, locating the forts has been the clue to finding the road which must have connected them.

South of Llanio, the Sarn Helen divides at Llanfair Clydogau, with the western branch leading to Carmarthen, probably closely followed by the present A485. The other branch led to Llandovery, going across the hills to Pumsaint, where the Roman fort which guarded the gold mines at Dolaucothi was discovered only in 1972, and thence via Caeo and Porthyrhyd to Llandovery; this route was to be used again by the drovers many centuries later (see Chapter 6).

High Street

High Street is probably the best-known Roman road in the Lake District; its route along the top of the mountain ridge of the same name is spectacular, keeping at a height of over 460m (1500ft) for some 10 miles (16km), and reaching almost 825m (2700ft) at the summit (Hindle, 1984). This central section of the route is very clear on the ground. From High Raise the road runs northwards in a straight line along the crest of the ridge to Loadpot Hill. Here it changes alignment, and aims directly for the fort at Brougham. There is a well defined agger, and much of this alignment runs closely parallel to a parish boundary (Figs. 20 and 21).

There are many difficulties associated with this route, however. Between the known northern end of the summit section and Brougham the evidence is very confusing, and no clear route has been found; much of this area has been enclosed, and more recently deep ploughed. To the south of the summit its course has never been established at all; its obvious destination would have been the fort at Ambleside, but a possible fort has recently been discovered at Broadgate, east of

21 *The agger of High Street at the northern end of the summit section; the course beyond to the fort at Brougham has not yet been found.*

22 *The confirmation of a Roman road over Kirkstone Pass, seen as the shelf on the right-hand side of the valley, has cast doubt on the importance of High Street, which lies only a few miles to the east.*

Windermere, at the very southern end of the High Street ridge. The question also has to be asked whether the Romans would have been able to use horses regularly on a road which has no water supplies for at least 10 miles (16km). The final doubt is caused by the discovery of a definite Roman road from Ambleside northwards over the Kirkstone Pass, along Ullswater, and then via Whitbarrow to Old Penrith (Fig. 22) (Richardson & Allan, 1990). Much of this route is only a few miles to the west of High Street, and, being much lower, has no lack of water. Why should there be two parallel Roman roads here?

Perhaps the answer is that High Street was simply an old ridgeway which the Romans improved in part, as an early temporary military link between Brougham and Ambleside; it would certainly have been an obvious route to choose. But in the long run

it was not needed, and never became an important route. The reason why the route at the southern end has not been found may well be that the Romans never engineered this section at all.

Kendal to Ravenglass

Like High Street, this route also traverses the Lakeland fells, but it could hardly be more different. We know that it was an important route as it is listed as the final two stages of a route in the *Antonine Itinerary*. It traverses difficult terrain, and there must have been compelling reasons for building it. The road may have been built to isolate the Britons of southern Lakeland (there are no known Roman roads or forts in Lakeland south of this line), or simply to complete the road network by providing a second link to the southernmost fort along the Cumbrian coast. The idea that it was built in preparation for an invasion of Ireland is no longer supported.

In terms of surviving field evidence, most of the route is totally unknown – only 8 miles (13km) out of the 33 miles (53km) have been identified on the ground (Hindle, 1984). A further short section of this route near Windermere been located in the past few years, running roughly from Ings through Broadgate towards Allen Knott.

The best surviving section is through the hills, over the two passes, where it can be followed almost continuously for 6 miles (10km) (Fig. 23). The road first appears on Wrynose Pass above the modern road, as a terrace on the hillside, up to 5.5m (18ft) wide. The two routes meet at the top of the pass, but then diverge, with the Roman road again above the present one. Once in Wrynose Bottom, the Roman road is very clear as a 7m (24ft) wide causeway on the north side of the stream, complete with kerb stones. Beyond Cockley Beck Bridge it is represented by the track to Black Hall. For the ascent of Hardknott Pass the Romans chose an entirely different route to the present road; their route is still a right of way, and is clearly shown on the OS map. It has a different summit, but the two roads join briefly for the start of the descent; however, where the modern road makes its notorious steep zigzag, the Romans went straight on, heading for their fort, perched high above Eskdale (Fig. 24). The road was engineered to a high standard; it was never less than 5m (15ft) wide, even in the most difficult places:

> it shows a considerable adaptation to the physical topography with cuttings, terraces, curves and straight alignments, all built to reduce to a minimum the considerable problems for road users. (Taylor, 1979.)

Below the fort, the Roman road disappears in the fields, and the rest of its route to Ravenglass is elusive.

---

23   *The Roman road over Hardknott and Wrynose passes is still clear on the ground, but the links to Ravenglass and Ambleside have proved elusive.*

24 *The Roman road descending the western side of Hardknott Pass went straight on at this point, heading for the fort. The parade ground above the fort can be seen in the middle distance, left.*

Other roads

This is a brief list of some of the other well known Roman roads, concentrating on those which have acquired specific names:

Ackling Dyke: Old Sarum (Salisbury) to Dorchester. A massive agger can be seen in several places, notably where the road crosses the Dorset Downs of Cranborne Chase. The well preserved agger south of Woodyates (10 miles (16km) south-west of Salisbury on the A354) is best observed on Bottlebush Down, where the Dyke is crossed by the B3081 (Fig. 25).

It is impossible to exaggerate, and indeed difficult adequately to describe, the magnificence which now lies ahead . . . One feels that one must be viewing the embankment of an abandoned main-line railway rather than a Roman road! (Margary, 1973.)

Johnston (1979) suggests that this was planned as a prestige road, but was little used, and proved to be a white elephant; indeed, one excavated section was found to have its metalling virtually intact.

Blackstone Edge: an impressive section of the road from Manchester to Ilkley, which crosses the Pennines at 450m (1475ft). It is a paved road which climbs straight up the hill above Littleborough at gradients of up to 1 in 4; the later packhorse track and two turnpike roads take much longer and less steep routes. This one of only five places in

25 *The massive agger of Ackling Dyke on Bottlebush Down, south-west of Salisbury, is one of the most impressive surviving Roman roads.*

27 *Dere Street is overlain by the A68 for most of the 18 miles (29km) north of Hadrian's Wall; there are numerous dire warnings to modern-day drivers.*

26 *The paved Roman road crossing the Pennines at Blackstone Edge above Littleborough has a central groove, possibly used for braking.*

Britain where a Roman road has a central line of stones; the curious feature here is that these stones have a deep groove, which is generally thought to have been created by the use of poles as brakes (Fig. 26). There has been much local controversy as to whether this is a Roman road at all!

Dere Street: from York to Corbridge and across the Cheviots into Scotland; much is still in use south of Hadrian's Wall (notably the A1 to Scotch Corner). Beyond the Wall many sections are still very clear; here the directness of this road over the hilly country has made the A68 into a notoriously dangerous switchback (Fig. 27).

Devil's Causeway: a branch from Dere Street just north of the Wall, leading to Berwick; its name derives from a Dark Age superstition about its origins. Most of it is

no longer used as a road, and little now remains.

Ermine Street: the main route from London via Godmanchester, Water Newton, Lincoln and the Humber estuary to York. It was laid out very skilfully at an early date, and has an overall directness similar to that of Watling Street and the Foss Way. Much of it is still a main road, notably many sections of the A1(M) north of London, but the section for 30 miles (48km) from Colsterworth north along the chalk ridge to Lincoln is now either a B road or simply a track: it is known here as High Dyke, and was later used as a drove road (Fig. 28). The section north of Lincoln is a magnificent stretch of road, still in use for most of the way to the Humber (A15 and B1207). As a route to York this section was replaced by the Great North Road which leads off to the west only 3 miles (5km) north of Lincoln, going via Doncaster and Tadcaster, thus avoiding the Humber crossing.

Icknield Way/Street: Romanized prehistoric route; see Chapter 2.

Peddars Way: From Ixworth to the Wash, where there was probably a ferry; it was the central part of the route from Colchester to Lincoln. It was a well-built road, but curiously runs parallel to the Icknield Way. It is now mostly a green lane or footpath, and has been designated as a long-distance path; the final 20 mile (32km) length from Castle Acre to Holme next the Sea is an excellent walk (Robinson, 1986).

28 *Ermine Street south of Lincoln ceased to be used as a road, but was later used by generations of drovers. It became known as High Dyke, and was finally incorporated in the enclosed field system.*

Via Devana: Colchester to Ermine Street (Godmanchester); the name is eighteenth century, based on the suggestion that it was the route to Chester (Deva). It survives as a green lane for 11 miles (18km) south-east of Cambridge; here it became known in the Middle Ages as Wool Street (originally Wolvestreet!).

Postscript

Following the collapse of Roman rule around AD 400, the roads were no longer maintained and many of those with minimal engineering simply disappeared back into the landscape. The major roads survived, and many remained in use, even though the new settlers shunned them when choosing sites for their settlements. Even at the end of the Dark Ages, after 600 years of total neglect, they were clearly still usable; at worst they were the easiest way across the country. From medieval times onwards, those which remained in use were altered to a greater or lesser extent. Some became rutted or were turned into holloways by the sheer pressure of traffic, while others were later improved as turnpike or enclosure roads. These improvements often obliterated what then remained of the original road, and more recently many have been regraded and covered with tarmac. Such changes will inevitably have destroyed much of the original structure of the Roman road, though later roads often diverted from the Roman line, either to pass through a village or town, or in order to take an easier gradient – here the old agger may still survive.

The importance of Roman roads in the growth of the road system of Britain is very great indeed, despite the fact that their roads and towns were imposed on the countryside, rather than growing from the demands of local people. Numerous Roman roads are still in use today, whether as main roads such as the A5, country lanes or simply as tracks or footpaths. There was to be no more large-scale road maintenance until 1555, and no more deliberate road construction until the improvement of the turnpikes in the early years of the nineteenth century.

4 Medieval routes

The Dark Ages

After the departure of the Romans and the demise of their political and economic systems, Britain entered what is popularly called the Dark Ages, a period which is dark because there is so little historical evidence of any kind. There was certainly much less trade and travel, and thus less need for roads. As for the prehistoric period, it is impossible to be at all precise about roads in the Dark Ages, save that the Roman roads clearly remained in use.

The Saxons had arrived in substantial numbers by the sixth century, and it used to be thought that they introduced the village to the British landscape. In fact, recent archaeological work has shown that most villages were not established until at least the eleventh century, and, until that date, most people lived only in individual farmsteads or in settlements no larger than hamlets. The typical layout of the Midlands village with its houses, church, fields and tracks emerged 500 years later than was traditionally thought. The northern and western parts of Britain never had villages imposed upon them, and the tracks and lanes which still run from one isolated farm or hamlet to the next may well have changed little over thousands of years.

Not enough is known about the overall pattern of Dark Age settlement to be able to say very much about the tracks which were in use. It appears that the sites on which the Saxons (and later the Danes) chose to live were usually away from Roman roads, presumably on the grounds that those routes would only bring trouble. As already noted, it is stunningly clear throughout the English Midlands that Roman roads often form the boundaries of parishes, rather than going through the settlements at their centres. If nothing else, their aggers and ditches provided clear and convenient dividing lines in the landscape.

Anglo-Saxon charters sometimes have clauses describing these boundaries, and thus may provide the earliest documentary evidence for roads (Hooke, 1977). Several words are commonly used: *Straet* usually refers to a Roman or paved road, whilst *paeth* and *weg* refer to tracks, the latter sometimes given more explicitly as *holanweg* (holloway; a road hollowed out by the passage of people and animals; Figs. 29 and 32). It is important to realize that the reference to a road as a boundary does not tell us whether the road was actually in use at the time.

The skeleton of the minor road system of Britain was created piecemeal over a very long period, simply through the needs of farmers to get to their fields and pasture, or to travel to neighbouring settlements. In some places the lanes may well be prehistoric in origin, elsewhere Roman, Saxon, Danish or medieval; certainly many rural tracks are of great antiquity. It is highly probable that the system of minor roads was

29 *The deeply entrenched holloway climbing up to White Sheet Hill from Shaftesbury has probably been used since prehistoric times. Traffic now follows the A30 in the valley below.*

essentially complete in terms of length by AD 1000, though it has continued to change its form ever since.

During the Dark Ages there were many warring factions, and from time to time certain routes were used by particular armies; these became known as 'herepaths' (army roads). A good example is the Salisbury Way, leading from Shaftesbury via White Sheet Hill and Chiselbury to Salisbury. Its origins are probably prehistoric, but it is mentioned as a herepath and boundary in two Anglo-Saxon charters, it was used as a drove road and eventually it became part of the main coach road to the west from Salisbury. It is now a quiet green lane (Figs. 29 and 30). The Wiltshire Herepath is another well-preserved trackway which runs from Marlborough to Avebury over Fyfield Down, but it too probably has prehistoric origins, effectively being a branch of the Great Ridgeway (see Fig. 3). It was also used until the eighteenth century as a coach road.

For most of this period there were probably no functioning towns and little trading, and thus even the Roman roads would have seen hardly any traffic. Trade did eventually start to grow again, notably in the years around the start of the ninth century, and this led to the naming of certain tracks as Port Ways, each leading to a

30 *The 'Salisbury Way' has probably been in use since prehistoric times. In the Dark Ages it was a herepath (army path), and later became a drove road and coach road.*

particular port or market town. These were usually prehistoric tracks or Roman roads being used again. Many continued to be called Port Ways during the medieval period. The *Anglo-Saxon Chronicle* mentions the Portway from Northampton to Southampton via Oxford, and a well-known example is the Roman road from Silchester to Old Sarum (Salisbury); it is no longer a through route, and its use near the abandoned Roman town of Silchester must have ceased early in Saxon times. In Derbyshire, a Portway can be traced from Nottingham to Wirksworth and Bakewell by a succession of documentary references and place-names (Dodd, 1980).

The Saxon struggle against the Danish invasion led to the creation of a network of fortified places (*būrhs*) by the early tenth century; the Danes also established boroughs. Many of these defended places, such as Wallingford, Shaftesbury, Wareham, Derby, Nottingham and Bedford attracted trade, and they mark the real

beginnings of medieval urban growth. They became important both as military and trading centres, and the old roads leading to them would have seen an increasing amount of traffic. The changes to the roads leading into Stamford, Winchester and Tamworth are outlined by Taylor (1979). At Stamford, the first Saxon settlement seems to have been away from the Roman road, almost half a mile downstream, near an easy fording point (Fig. 31). In the late ninth century the Danes built a fort close by, and when the area was reconquered by the English thirty years later, they built a new *būrh* on the opposite side of the river. The place where the main road crossed the river simply moved downstream in response to the changing settlement pattern.

Medieval main roads

By the early eleventh century political control had been steadily consolidated, and a single English kingdom had emerged. At

31 *The road pattern at Stamford changed during the Dark Ages in response to the changing settlement sites of the Saxons, Danes and then English. (After Taylor, 1979.)*

the same time the medieval trading system was growing. Trade was inextricably linked with urban growth, because most trading was conducted in towns, immune from the new restrictions of feudalism. At the time of the Domesday Survey (1086) there were probably only about 50 places in England with genuine urban features and functions, yet by the early fourteenth century, there were between five and six hundred towns, and most had grown considerably in size.

As a general rule, those towns which were located on major routes or at important junctions prospered, whilst others situated or deliberately planted even only a short distance from a road, often failed to grow. Examples of the failures include Church Brough (Cumbria), superseded by Market Brough on the main road less than half a mile away, and Beaudesert (Warwickshire) which was replaced by Henley in Arden, less than 180m (600ft) distant. Sometimes long-established roads were deliberately diverted or new bridges built so that traffic had to pass through a town's market place; this happened at St Ives (Cambridgeshire), Boroughbridge, Thame (Oxford) and Montacute (Somerset). At Ludlow the building of a new bridge across the Teme early in the thirteenth century achieved the same result. The study of streets within towns is a fascinating one, though outside the scope of this book (Hindle, 1990).

Many towns also had access to rivers and the sea; it is important to remember that many heavy or bulky goods were transported to and then by water wherever possible, even if our concern here is only with the roads.

The growth of towns has been well studied, but precisely how goods were moved from one place to another, and, more importantly, what routes were used and what was the nature of the resulting road network, are topics which have been given very little attention. This curious omission is almost certainly due to the paucity of the available evidence; relatively few direct records of such commonplace activities as travel and trade survive. It used to be thought that few people travelled beyond their own manor at this time, but this was clearly not the case. Most peasants would have travelled regularly to the local market or county town, and there were many other travellers such as workmen, minstrels, messengers, bishops, preachers and friars, pardoners, pilgrims, justices, taxmen and outlaws, quite apart from the all important merchants (Jusserand, 1889). The road system was a vital and integral part of the whole medieval economy, and, as such, deserves more study than it has so far received.

Sources

The sources for the study of medieval roads are varied. The remains of the roads and tracks themselves, whether seen from the ground or from aerial photographs, can be difficult to interpret; it is impossible by archaeological methods to date a road which has not been deliberately constructed, even if the remains are substantial. In physical terms, most medieval roads would have been packhorse tracks, though the major routes must have been capable of taking wagons. These often became sunken roads or 'holloways', because of the erosion caused by the traffic, made worse by the rain (Fig. 32). A common feature is the spreading

32 *The steep holloway running down from the deserted medieval village of Richard's Castle, south of Ludlow, now sees very little traffic.*

out and duplication of tracks where a route left cultivated land, or where a hill had to be climbed. Many such rutted holloways are described as being medieval, but their origins may either lie far earlier, or even later.

The building and repairing of bridges was regarded as a pious act in medieval times, and is quite well recorded; special taxes (pontages) could also be levied. Sometimes a new bridge altered the whole pattern of traffic in an area, with consequences far away. For example, the building of Harnham Bridge south of the new town of Salisbury in 1244 diverted traffic from Wilton which had formerly been the major town in the area. Equally, the building of the bridge at Abingdon probably contributed to the decline of Dorchester on Thames and even Wallingford. The new twelfth-century bridge over the Ure at Boroughbridge diverted the course of the Great North Road, so that it crossed the river half a mile upstream, at the new town. The old Roman road degenerated into a grassy lane, and finally ceased to be a road altogether when the area was enclosed in 1809. Causeways were effectively extended bridges across marshes or wide rivers. Maud Heath's Causeway near Chippenham is one of the more substantial and unusual examples; it is 4½ miles (7km) in length, and was built soon after 1474, enabling people to cross the river Avon dry-shod. The causeways across the Fens to Ely may well also be medieval, they were certainly being extensively maintained and improved at this time.

The best evidence for medieval roads comes from those documentary sources which show that someone actually travelled along a particular road. The itineraries of the medieval monarchs are the most detailed records, giving a day-to-day record of the movements of the king and of his household, from the time of King John onwards. These early monarchs were itinerant – John moved over 13 times a month on average throughout his reign, in both summer and winter. Thus we have an invaluable record, even if the kings travelled to some places which the ordinary traveller would not visit. Moving the paraphernalia of the royal household (including the chancery and exchequer) required up to twenty carts and wagons, and reasonable roads were clearly needed. There are also a few surviving records of the movement of goods; the best are those kept by the government when buying food to provision armies abroad. With bulky goods such as grain, it is clear that rivers were used wherever possible. Some monastic and estate records also give details of the movement of goods, but rarely of the precise routes taken.

There is an increasing number of documents as the medieval period progressed, whether of local, legal, monastic or national origin, which can be used to identify stretches of road. A whole host of words in various languages are used to refer to roads: the Saxon *paeth*, *straet* and *weg*, give way to the Latin *strata* and *via*, and the English gate and highway, among many others. There were also more complex descriptions such as *via regia*, *magna via*, or *stayngate* (stony road – usually a later description of a Roman road). A selection from Derbyshire includes *Viam Comitis* (the Earl's Way), Broad Gate, Castlegate, Peakway and Alsopeway (the way to Alsop). In Wales and the Welsh borders, road place-name elements include *ffordd*, *heol* and *sarn*. Road name evidence should not be relied on uncritically; for example, a road might have been given a name out of ignorance or superstition. A herepath may never have been trodden by an army, and a *via regia* may never have seen a king, though such a name implies a certain degree of importance for a road.

There are also a number of court cases concerning roads, such as that against the

33 *East Anglia as shown on the Gough Map. The road from London to Norwich, plus part of the Great North Road are clearly shown, together with distances between the towns. The map is probably late thirteenth century. East is at the top.*

Abbot of Chertsey in 1386, who had allowed two 'wells' to exist in the high road from Egham to Staines. The Abbot was in court, not for failing to maintain the road, but because a hapless man had drowned in one of the holes, and the Abbot had claimed his goods. Elsewhere, men were prosecuted for ploughing up roads, planting hedges too close and even for erecting buildings on the highway. The wholly negative evidence given by such cases is probably not representative of the general condition of most roads. The fact that the kings and their entourage managed to travel throughout the year suggests that the roads were in a reasonable state.

There is a further important legal point:

the medieval concept of a road was that it was a right of way, or an 'easement', rather than a physical entity. Thus if a section was foundrous or impassible, the traveller had the right to diverge from it, even to the extent of trampling crops. This may well be the root cause of some of the twists and turns in many country lanes which can still be seen today.

Perhaps the most important single source of information about the main roads is the

34 *The transportation system of medieval England, the major towns were linked to each other by both road and river.*

Gough Map, probably first drawn in the late thirteenth century, and revised in about 1360, which shows a network of almost 3000 miles (4800km) of roads in England and Wales (Fig. 33). London is clearly the centre of a network of roads radiating out to all parts of the kingdom. Even where roads are not shown, the towns *en route* are usually

Major road
Navigable river
● Prominent medieval borough

0   50 miles

shown correctly. About 40 per cent of the routes shown are on the lines of Roman roads, whereas the rest were the new medieval roads which made and maintained themselves simply through the continual passage of traffic.

It is possible to make a number of general statements about the network of major roads in medieval times (Hindle, 1989). First, many Roman roads remained in use, still providing the easiest way across the country. Second, new medieval roads came into being simply through habitual use. Third, the road system as a whole was adequate for the amount of traffic that existed, even in winter. Fourth, roads often acted as feeders to the river system for the movement of heavy or bulky merchandise. Finally, it is clear that many of today's major roads were created or used in the medieval period, simply because of the need to service the great growth in medieval agriculture, industry and trade. Of course, many routes simply reused earlier trackways. By the end of the medieval period there was a well-integrated transport network, well capable of serving the needs of the economy (Fig. 34).

Clearly, many of the types of road described in following chapters were in use in medieval times. Drove roads have their origins in this period, as do many trading routes such as 'saltways'; all these became much more important later and are dealt with in Chapters 6 and 7.

A few of the county studies in 'The Making of the English Landscape' series stress the importance of roads in the development of the medieval landscape; of particular note are those of Northamptonshire by Steane (1974) and of Hertfordshire by Munby (1977). An introduction to the evidence for medieval roads in Scotland is given in Fenton and Stell (1984).

35 *Medieval roads in Cambridgeshire. (After Taylor, 1979.)*

Local studies

Local studies of medieval routes may look at major or minor roads; they may take a specific road, or try to reconstruct the road network of a particular area, whether a single parish, or a whole county. Examples can be found for Derbyshire in Dodd (1980), for the Yorkshire Dales in Wright (1985), for the Lake District in Hindle (1984) and for Northamptonshire and elsewhere in Taylor

(1979). All show how detailed historical study together with field observation can produce excellent results. Taylor gives an interesting example in Cambridgeshire, showing how the routes along the line of Ermine Street altered during the medieval period (Fig. 35). Here the Roman road seems to have been abandoned for drier routes to the west, notably through Coppingford and Ogerston, neither of which now survives as a village. This route is no longer a through route, as the A1 has largely reverted to the Roman line.

Many features in the landscape are not fixed, but are in a continual state of evolution and change. The local road network is no exception, evolving to serve the changing pattern of settlement, just as the major road network changed as towns grew and prospered. Virtually the only place where it is possible to find a guaranteed 'medieval road' (i.e. one which was not in existence before or used since) is where a road leads to the site of a village created and then deserted in the medieval period, or one leading to a failed medieval new town.

At the parish level there were numerous tracks leading from the farms and villages to fields, pasture and woodland, and it is all too easy to forget them in looking at the more important routes. Indeed, these tracks have rarely been studied in any detail. Very often, they can be glimpsed in early estate plans, for although the earliest of these were not drawn until the late sixteenth century, they often still show much of the medieval layout. A map of Padbury (Buckinghamshire), drawn in 1591 depicts numerous irregular tracks leaving the village, their main function being to give access to the fields; many do not even reach the parish boundary (Fig. 36). Most such field tracks have been destroyed by later ploughing or by enclosure (see Chapter 9). However, where the ridge and furrow pattern of medieval fields still survives, the unploughed headlands which gave access

and a turning place for the plough, and the holloways leading to the next village can often still be traced.

Even where the physical remains have been totally removed, there may be other map evidence in pre-enclosure or tithe maps, even though these may be as late as the mid-nineteenth century in date, and thus somewhat remote from the medieval period (Hindle, 1988). It should also be remembered that many field tracks go back much further than the medieval period, having their origins in Roman or prehistoric times.

In areas where arable cultivation was not the norm, fields and the tracks leading to them might be very irregular, both being created piecemeal as needed. Any upland area of western Britain such as the Lake District or Dartmoor has such tracks, and beyond the enclosed area, tracks lead out on to the moors; each Lakeland village has its own section of fell, the two being connected by various tracks along which the sheep and cattle would be driven. Areas brought into cultivation from other types of waste land such as forest or fen also had their access routes. However, unless there is documentary evidence, it is difficult to date any of these tracks.

Church paths and corpse roads

A few tracks were used principally for access to the parish church. Sometimes documentary evidence survives; in the accounts of the Bailiff of the Forest of Dartmoor for 1491, a parcel of land is described as bounded by a 'Churchway' to Widecombe (Hemery, 1986). In the extreme south-west of Cornwall (West Penwith) these ways have been identified as 'church paths', many of which are named as such in documents, often in the Cornish equivalent, 'forth eglos' (usually shortened to 'freglos') (Maxwell, 1976). In medieval times, this

Open field area

Leaes

Stighgate
Waye

Forde

HEDGE FIELD

Whadden
Waye

St. Katherne's Waye

Buckingham
Waye

Whadden Waye

Turninge Slade

Pinnocke Slade

Back Lane

Old End

Back Lane

EAST FIELD

Mylne

Norburye

WEST FIELD

Bradmore Meadowe

Forde

White Bridge

Forde

0   yards   440

area had only 13 parish churches, and church paths led to them from outlying farmsteads up to 3 miles (5km) away. Many of the paths were marked by granite wayside crosses. Over a hundred of these crosses remain, though others have been lost and are represented only by field names.

Rather better known are the corpse roads which were used for taking the dead from isolated farms or hamlets to the parish church for burial. These roads were usually little more than packhorse tracks, as most coffins would have been carried on horseback. They are best seen in the more remote areas of the country where the parishes are large and most farmsteads lie far from the church. The different names for such roads around the country include coffin roads, kirk roads and lich or lych ways (lich is an old word for a corpse). There is often little documentary evidence of their use; indeed it may be nothing more than local tradition.

Robertson (1947) describes several such tracks in the Highlands of Scotland, including routes from Glen Strath Farrar to Kintail, from Quoich Bridge to Glen Shiel, and from Glen Garry to Glen Moriston. Less than 10 miles (16km) south of Edinburgh, a 'kirk road' runs from Bavelaw and Loganlee across the pass between Carnethy and Scald Law (the highest point of the Pentland Hills) to the church at Penicuik.

Examples in northern England include a corpse road which runs from Garrigill (in the South Tyne valley above Alston) for 11 miles (18km), reaching a height of almost 800m (2600ft) on Cross Fell, before descending to the mother church at Kirkland in the Eden valley. Only a few miles to the

south there is a parallel route from Birkdale in Upper Teesdale, which runs for 12 miles (20km), passing through the great gash of High Cup to the parish church at Dufton. The track through the chasm is known as Narrowgate, and the whole route is still in use as it is now followed by the Pennine Way. Further south, in Swaledale, bodies were carried in wicker baskets from the area around Keld at the top of the dale, for over 12 miles (20km) to the church at Grinton, until a burial ground was provided at Muker in 1580. In Derbyshire, the dead from Edale were taken over Hollins Cross for burial in Castleton until 1633.

The Lake District also has several corpse roads; one led from the village of Mardale Green (now usually submerged beneath Haweswater) to the mother church at Shap, some 7 miles (11km) distant (Fig. 37). Leaving the village it climbs steeply via a series of zigzags on to Mardale Common, reaching 500m (1656ft), it then descends into the little visited valley of Swindale, and finally crosses the moor to the church where it is known as the Kirk Gate (i.e. Church Road). The chapel at Mardale was granted its own burial ground in 1728, and the last corpse was taken to Shap in 1736. Another Lakeland example is the remote track across Burnmoor, which connects the tiny hamlet of Wasdale Head with St Catherine's church at Boot, over 6 miles (10km) away.

Much the same conditions led to the creation of a Lich Way across Dartmoor, as all those who died within the area of the ancient Forest of Dartmoor had be buried at Lydford until 1260. The people worst affected were those who lived in the centre of the moor, only a few miles from the church at Widecombe. Instead, they had to take corpses across the moor, climbing to a height of over 460m (1500ft). Here weather conditions could be so bad that the direct route to Lydford could not be used, and roundabout routes had to be taken instead, which were often twice as long. There are

---

36 *Medieval tracks in Padbury (Buckinghamshire) as shown on an estate plan of 1591; most simply gave access to the fields and did not reach the parish boundary.*

37 *The villagers of Mardale Green carried their dead for burial over the fells to Shap until 1736. The remains of the village are normally submerged beneath Haweswater.*

several possible routes across the moor from Two Bridges, Bellever and Postbridge; they traverse the southern slopes of Cut Hill, and cross the Tavy near Wapsworthy, 3 miles (5km) short of Lydford (Toulson, 1984; Hemery, 1986).

Pilgrim routes

In a more pious age than our own, it was common for people to travel to visit the various shrines dotted around the country, as well as those abroad. In England, the shrine of St Swithun at Winchester was much visited, and pilgrims also travelled to remote places such as Hereford to seek a particular saint's aid. But the principal pilgrim destinations were the long established chapel of Our Lady of Walsingham, and later the shrine of Thomas à Becket in Canterbury, set up after his murder in 1170.

At the start of *The Canterbury Tales*, written in about 1400, Chaucer says that once April comes,

Thanne longen folk to goon on pilgrimages . . .
And specially from every shires ende
Of Engelond to Caunterbury they wende

His pilgrims travelled from Southwark, and only five places en route are mentioned (Depeford, Grenewych, Sidyngborne, Boghtoun under Blee and Bobbe-up-and-doun; the last is probably Harbledown). Although Chaucer uses the pilgrimage to string together a set of tales, he takes it for granted that his readers know the road, and he never mentions any difficulties of travel. We may assume that this Roman road was probably still in a reasonable state of repair. This was surely the most important single pilgrim route in later medieval England; the road was equally important as part of the main road to Dover and thence to France.

One particular route has become known as the 'Pilgrims' Way' (Jennett, 1971). It runs along the North Downs, beginning at Winchester, and proceeds via Alton to Farnham, then along the Hog's Back past Guildford, then to Dorking, Titsey, Wrotham, Snodland, Charing and finally to Canterbury. In fact this is probably a route of much greater antiquity and importance, its use long pre-dating the coming of pilgrims. Hilaire Belloc (1910) called it the Old Road, and it is a typical ridgeway route (see Chapter 2). It may well have provided a route to and from the great ceremonial centres of Salisbury Plain. The original route from Stonehenge passed where Andover and Basingstoke now stand, and joined the Pilgrims' Way at Farnham; this older route is known as the Harrow Way (see Fig. 2). Several Roman villas appear to be connected with the Pilgrims' Way, though there is no evidence of the route being improved by the Romans.

Unfortunately, there is no real evidence for the use of this route by medieval pilgrims and the first mention of this romantic idea dates from the eighteenth century. In any case, the traffic of pilgrims lasted for less than four hundred years, and the track probably has its origins some three and a half thousand years ago. No doubt some pilgrims did use it, but its main users would have been drovers and traders, especially in the eighteenth century when they were trying to avoid the tolls of the newly turnpiked roads. It is always dubious to name a track after one particular type of user; only rarely was any road used for a single purpose.

Nevertheless, the passage of men and animals over thousands of years has created a very clear series of tracks and holloways along this route. Sometimes the route runs on top of the ridge, but more frequently it appears as a terraceway on the scarp slope, as parts of the chalk ridge are topped with clay-with-flints which would have been hard going in wet conditions. Some sections are overlain by modern roads, whilst others remain as tracks or paths. It has been an important through-route for thousands of years, and the 'Old Road' is certainly a better name for it. More recently, the North Downs Way has been established as one of the many long-distance footpaths; its route has been chosen to avoid motor roads as much as possible, and only coincides in places with the various lines of the Old Road or the Pilgrims' Way (Herbstein, 1982).

Monastic routes

There are many tracks with monastic connections which may appear at first sight to have a medieval origin. One such is the so-called Abbots' Way across southern Dartmoor which appears to connect Buckfast Abbey with the abbeys at Tavistock and Buckland. However, the track is certainly older than the abbeys, and although the monks no doubt used it, it was always known as the Jobbers' Path or Cawse until a traveller called John Andrews first dubbed it the Abbots' Way in 1794. In fact a parallel route some miles further north across the moor, which is marked with 22 stone crosses, appears to be a much better

38   *The monastic route of Mastiles Lane in winter, crossing Malham Moor at a height of almost 400m (1300ft).*

candidate as a monastic route; however, there is no direct evidence of monks using this track either (Peel, 1971; Groves, 1972; Toulson, 1983; Hemery, 1986).

Rather more successful has been the detailed investigation of the numerous routes connected with Strata Florida Abbey in Cardiganshire by Colyer (1984). The Welsh place-names include an abbey road, pilgrims' ford and monk's way. Colyer's study was backed up by detailed field observation and historical research.

In the Yorkshire Dales the most famous surviving monastic road is probably Mastiles Lane, which was originally known as Strete Gate. It runs from Kilnsey (a grange or farm of Fountains Abbey) westwards across Malham Moor, heading for Ribblesdale and Clapham, and eventually for the Abbey's distant estates in the Lake District. Rights of passage were granted to the abbey's men, animals and goods throughout its length. Originally it was an unwalled track across the open moors, marked by crosses at prominent points; several of their bases are still in place.

Mastiles Lane continued to be used by the drovers, driving their cattle from Scotland (see Chapter 6). When the whole area was eventually enclosed in the late eighteenth and early nineteenth centuries, it and numerous other drovers' routes were constrained between new walls which were built sufficiently far apart to allow easy passage for the herds of cattle. It is now one of the many Green Lanes of the Pennines (Fig. 38)

The high medieval period was brought to a sudden end by the arrival of the Black Death in 1348, which cut the population by 40 per cent. Some villages began to be deserted as a result of the fall in population, and their roads went out of use. Plague became endemic, and for almost a century and a half, the economy barely prospered, a situation exacerbated by the Wars of the Roses. The amount of trade and traffic fell significantly, and once again there is little record of the road system; it almost certainly failed to grow until political and economic conditions improved in the sixteenth century.

5 Early modern roads

With the re-establishment of firm central government by Henry VII in 1485, there began a period of sustained economic growth, which has lasted, with only a few minor setbacks, until the present day. This chapter is essentially concerned with roads in the sixteenth and seventeenth centuries.

The monasteries had undertaken some maintenance of bridges and roads throughout the medieval period, and travellers rarely complained about the roads. John Leland was the first traveller to write about his travels. Around 1540 he visited most of the monasteries and makes frequent reference to bridges and river crossings, but says little about the roads, implying that most were in a reasonable condition. The dissolution of the monasteries in the late 1530s was one of Henry VIII's more drastic actions, and it may well be that the removal of the limited road repair undertaken by the monasteries, plus the growing amount of traffic, began to put strains on the road system. Another factor was that the climate was changing from the drier and warmer conditions of the medieval period towards the so-called 'Little Ice Age' with its wetter and cooler summers and colder winters. This too must have contributed to the rapid deterioration of the roads which became evident in the late sixteenth century.

The surviving sections of the Roman road system still formed the backbone of the main road system, but during the medieval period many local roads had also become part of this system, and were particularly vulnerable to the damage caused by the ever increasing traffic. During the reign of Elizabeth I, the fine balance between the amount of traffic and the roads' ability to maintain themselves was evidently broken. Soon, references to poor and impassable roads, and to the difficulty of travelling in winter, became progressively more frequent (Crofts, 1967). In 1586, William Harrison complained that some highways

within these five and twentie yeares have beene in most places fiftie foot broad according to the law, whereby the traveller might . . . passe by the loaden cart without danger of himself and his horsse; now they are brought unto twelve, or twentie, or six and twentie at the most.

Moreover, travel in winter in some areas was a particular problem:

in the claie or cledgie soile they are often verie deepe and troublesome in the winter halfe.

Such comments were echoed by Camden, Speed, Pepys, Thoresby and Fiennes, among many others, during the seventeenth century. In the *Pilgrim's Progress* Bunyan uses the poor condition of so many roads as the model for the Slough of Despond.

The deterioration of the roads meant that the first English road legislation had to be passed in 1555, requiring each parish to repair all its own roads. Under earlier Common Law, a parish could be indicted for failing to repair its roads, but the new act was designed to promote regular road maintenance throughout the country. Parishioners were obliged to spend four days a year working on the roads, supervised by two surveyors appointed by the parish. As early as 1563 this was increased to six days, the surveyors were given stronger powers and the Justices were allowed to fine parishes which failed to maintain their roads. The statute was amended again in 1575 to allow the Justices to levy rates in order to repair particular roads. This was the beginning of a long series of Acts of Parliament concerning roads. For example, in 1691 minimum widths were laid down, namely 8ft (2.4m) for roads to market towns, and 3ft (1m) for horse causeys, whilst from 1697 signposts could be required to be erected. This legislative process eventually culminated in the eighteenth-century turnpike acts (see Chapter 8). It was not until the General Highway Act of 1835 that the 1555 Act was repealed.

In theory, the parish repair system was a reasonable solution to the problem, so long as there was little long distance through traffic, but in practice it did not work well. There were many weaknesses in the new system; the surveyors were essentially conscripted amateurs who were forced to do the job and to supervise unwilling labourers, many of whom never used the roads and thus had no interest in doing good work. Eventually, the six days of statute labour began to look like a holiday. The surveyors were appointed for only one year, were not paid, yet could be fined for negligence. There were a few keen exceptions, such as Benjamin Browne, sometime High Constable of Kendal, who undertook two surveys of his local roads in 1730–1. He had nothing good to say about any of them; most were described as narrow, bad and covered with hedges.

To make matters worse, some parishes had much more road to repair than others,

some had a busy main road to maintain, whilst others had a small population unable to cope. But even if the full amount of labour was obtained, the known repair methods were very rudimentary, usually consisting of little more than applying gravel to the surface, or digging ditches:

The nub of the matter was simply drainage. The worst roads suffered by virtue of the subsoil, by lack of any camber, by excessive gradients, by flooding, and by becoming so deeply rutted and pot-holed that the slightest deterioration in the weather made them into a morass. (Dyos & Aldcroft, 1969.)

It is hardly surprising that road repair by statute labour produced poor results. Essentially the problem was whether road users, local communities or the country as a whole should pay for the upkeep of roads. In fact, the successful improvement of road surfaces had to wait until the early nineteenth century and introduction of the techniques of McAdam, which were to be applied first to the turnpikes (see Chapter 8).

Until then the net result was roads which were often in an appalling state. This might be expected in the wetter and more hilly areas of the north and west, but roads near London were often just as bad, notably those across the Wealden clays. Late in the eighteenth century Horace Walpole wrote to a friend:

If you love good roads . . . be so kind as never to go into Sussex . . . Coaches grow there no more than balm or spices.

If the roads could not be adequately maintained, then the other way to improve matters was to try to restrict the carts, and especially the new wagons that were first mentioned in 1564. These became increasingly numerous on the roads from the late sixteenth century and were soon joined by private coaches, and then by stage-coaches in the first half of the next century. As early as 1621, Parliament tried to control the maximum weight of vehicles, especially in winter, or to restrict the number of horses, all to no avail. Once the roads had become deeply rutted, narrow wheels travelled best, but Parliament also tried from time to time to insist on broad wheels which it was thought would not only do less damage to the roads, but might also actually help to improve them. However, many wainwrights made matters worse by adding cogs to their narrow-rimmed wheels, which cut up the road surface even more, making it difficult for any other type of traffic to pass.

By 1660 there were regular coach services from London to the south-west, Lancashire, Newcastle and Edinburgh, and by 1705 some 180 towns had stage-coach services. Away from the main routes, however, the adoption of wagons and coaches spread only slowly from the area immediately around London. Beyond south-eastern England, wheeled traffic was rare, and most goods were moved by packhorse (Crofts, 1967). For example, Ralegh wrote in 1593 that it was impossible to take ordnance by land to Plymouth, whilst as late as 1749, a traveller observed that there was not one cart in the whole of Northumberland. The Weald had particular problems due to its heavy clays; an eighteenth-century gun founder had dragged twenty 9-foot-long 9-pounders to Lewes; he reported that they had:

torn the roads so that nothing can follow them and the [people of the] country curse us heartily.

Even Manchester and Liverpool were linked to each other only by packhorse routes until 1760. Thus narrow packhorse tracks were the norm throughout most of Britain; these 'pack and prime ways' were obviously cheaper to maintain than a full-width wagon or cart road. It comes as something of a surprise to realize that most parts of Britain did not have roads fit for wheeled vehicles until the late eighteenth century. Another problem was that travellers and carriers also had to contend

39 *An extract from a page of Ogilby's* Britannia *(1675) showing the road from Clapton to Oakham, plus numerous side roads and much other detail for the traveller.*

with robbers and highwaymen, not only in remoter areas, but also around London where rich pickings were to be had.

The postal system has its origins in the reign of Henry VIII and the first Postmaster-General was appointed by Elizabeth I; all official letters and parcels were carried by horse, and at first they were all routed through London (Crofts, 1967). Non-official items had to be sent with drovers or carriers, whether by packhorse, cart or wagon. The important Holyhead mail route, allowing communication with Ireland, was well established by 1600; it used the route along the coast of North Wales. The Milford Haven post route was established soon after, it went by way of Cardiff, Swansea and Haverfordwest. The official postal service began to carry private mail from 1635. In 1663, letters from London to Derby took three days, but by 1711, the same time allowed letters to reach Edinburgh, at a cost of 6d (2½p). Various cross-country routes were added during the seventeenth century, so that a comprehensive system of 'post-roads' emerged, together with Stage Towns and Branch Posts. There was nothing which made the post roads special other than the fact that mails were routinely carried along them. They are, however, an indication of the steadily growing economy and the need for good communications.

Ogilby and Fiennes

The seventeenth century provides the first detailed cartographic evidence for roads on a national scale. The earliest county maps, produced by Saxton (1570s) and Speed (1612) did not show roads, but a list of the principal highways was given by William Harrison in his *Description of Britain* in 1586. However, almost a century later, John Ogilby's *Britannia* (1675) undertook to illustrate the country

By a Geographical and Historical DESCRIPTION of the Principal Roads thereof. Actually Admeasured and Delineated in a Century of Whole-Sheet *Copper-Sculps.*

Two hundred pages of text were interleaved with the hundred road maps, based on surveys carried out over the previous six years. It was a pioneering work, and it was to be over a century before it was superseded (Hindle, 1988). Ogilby's road maps are an invaluable source, giving great detail of the main roads as well as of many minor roads.

Ogilby depicted each route in a series of scrolls, working across each page from bottom left to top right (Fig. 39). The roads are shown by solid lines where enclosed, and by dotted lines where they cross open country; down the centre of the roads are dots marking each quarter-mile or furlong, and the running mileage is also indicated. Numerous features on or near the roads such as bridges, rivers, castles, woods and churches are shown, all intended to help the traveller on his way. Steep hills are shown pictorially, with a hill indicating an ascent, and an upside-down hill a descent. These strip maps use a scale of one inch to the mile and thereby helped popularize the statute mile (it had been defined in 1593, though customary miles continued in use in many parts of the country for many years).

The total road system depicted by Ogilby is substantial; it owes much to the roads built by the Romans some one and a half thousand years before. In effect he shows a network which consists of eleven main roads leading from London to the provinces, linked by many cross-roads. Alternative routes are also given (some are described as 'worst' ways), and many side routes are indicated (Fig. 40). Ogilby's work was much copied, both in strip form and by adding his roads to county maps; this latter process began almost immediately, but the first complete set of county maps with roads was not produced until 1695 by Morden.

Barwick
Chapelburn   Haltwesell
Brampton   Newcastle
Warwick   Milton
Carlisle
Warwick   Corbey
Harrabey   Codby
Thursby   Carlton
Wickton   War Hesket
Old Carlisle   Hesket
Bothel   Rosley
Strictland Torpeny   Lasenbey
Ireby   Salkeldes
Bridkirk   Hutton
Papcastle   Penrith
Brigham Cockermouth
Eglesfield Bassenthwaite
            St.Johns
Whithaven Keswick   Applebey
            Thrumby Strickland
Wythbourn   Shap
Cleater Dunmail Raise
Egremond Grasmere
            Ambleside
            Stanlay
            Barnside
                Kendal
            Sidwick

            Betham
                Burton
            Carnford
Hest Bank
            Lancaster

—— Main route
— — Alternative 'worst way'
- - - - Other indicated route

0   Miles   10

40 *The network of roads in Cumbria shown in Ogilby's road book is far greater than the four main routes which are given in detail.*

Ogilby's work became progressively out of date as the turnpikes were established; it was eventually replaced by a new survey, published as Cary's *New Itinerary* in 1798, much copied by contemporary cartographers.

The most detailed records of travel in the years around 1700 are those left by Celia Fiennes, an early 'curious traveller' who travelled widely on horseback throughout England (Fiennes, 1982) (Fig. 41). The writings of this early tourist illustrate graphically the poor state of the roads on the very eve of the turnpike mania. It is difficult to choose from the many references she makes to the roads, most of which are not complimentary. Towards Plymouth she reported that

the wayes now became so difficult that one could

scarcely pass by each other, even the single horses.

Travelling to Ely, the ways were

very deep its mostly lanes and low moorish ground . . . on each side deffended by the fendiks [fen dykes] . . . and so you pass a flatt on a gravel Causey . . . In the winter this Causey is over flowed.

Near Bath there was a

narrow Causy that a Coach can scarce pass, all pitched with slatts and stones . . . its made only for Packhorses . . . the wayes to Bath are all difficult . . . its steep ascents all ways out of the town.

As we have already seen, the Sussex roads were notorious; the road from Tunbridge to London via Sevenoaks was

a sad deep clay way after wett.

Occasionally she reports good roads, sometimes going through parks on private roads, as at Leighton Hall north of Lancaster:

had the advantage of going through parke and saved the going round a bad stony passage . . . on to the road againe much of which was stony and steep, far worse than the Peake in Darbyshire.

She describes the strings of packhorses which were still much commoner on the roads than wagons, especially away from London:

abundance of horses I see all about Kendall streetes with their burdens.

She notes that many roads could not take wheeled vehicles at all:

The reason is plaine, from the narrowness of the

41 *The travels of Celia Fiennes; this curious traveller left little of England unvisited and wrote much about the roads on which she travelled.*

**Map legend:**

- - - - ○ - - - - *1697 journey*
━━━━━○━━━━━ *1698 'Great Journey'*
━━━━•━━━━ *Other journeys*

0 _____ miles _____ 50

NT *Newton Toney*
S *Salisbury*
W *Windsor*
Wi *Winchester*

0 — miles — 25

lanes where is good lands . . . and where its hilly and stoney no other carriages can pass.

This last description is of the road from Kendal to Windermere, which she says was capable of taking only narrow horse carts like wheel-barrows. Carriages simply could not travel along this road which appears on Ogilby's strip maps to be an important through route.

Finally she encountered the basic problems such as obtaining food and lodging, looking after her horses, and even finding the correct route:

if you take a wrong Way there is no passing – you are forced to have Guides as in all parts of Darbyshire

This was also true of many other parts of northern England, despite the fact that a law ordaining that signposts be erected had been passed in 1697.

In different ways, Ogilby and Fiennes sum up the situation on the roads at the end of the seventeenth century. On the one hand there was a network of roads covering the country, on which an increasing number of carriers was operating; but on the other, many lengths of road were narrow, steep or poorly maintained. Overall, packhorses remained the commonest means of transport, simply because wagons and coaches could not pass along such a number roads. The situation was, however, beginning to change, simply because trade was continuing to grow, and road improvements were being made; the first few turnpikes had already been enacted, and, as mentioned, one of the 1690s Highways Acts laid down minimum widths for different types of road.

Before turning to look in detail at the turnpikes, which marked such a fundamental change in the history of British roads, several special types of roads need some attention. The next two chapters will therefore deal with drove roads and packhorse tracks, and with various unusual roads.

6 Drove roads and packhorse tracks

Drove roads

The droving of cattle and sheep goes back into antiquity, probably starting with the transhumance movement of cattle and sheep between upland and lowland pastures. But from medieval times onwards, the long-distance droving trade grew steadily, reaching its zenith between the seventeenth to the mid-nineteenth centuries (Bonser, 1970; Toulson, 1980). In general, animals were driven from the wetter northern and western areas of Britain to the growing towns of England. Scotland and Wales were the two main sources of cattle, and most sheep came from Wales, though animals came from many other parts of the country too. Often the animals were kept for several months to be fattened at places along the drove roads where there was good grazing.

As with all migrations, the routes which were taken became standardized; not only out of habit and to take advantage of known facilities *en route*, but also because of the constraints of other features in the landscape. In hilly areas, there are obvious controls on the routes the cattle could take, but in the lowlands their routes were also constrained by the growing population and the ever increasing number of enclosed fields. Sometimes these new fields encroached on traditional drove roads, and the drovers were often forced to keep to higher ground. They disliked travelling along newly walled, hedged or fenced roads through enclosed land, as there was little wayside forage for the cattle.

Drove roads are sometimes referred to as driftways, a 'drift' simply being another word for a 'drive' or 'drove'. Today they are also often called green roads, though this term can include almost any old track now not covered by tarmac; the classic study of these roads in the Pennines is by Raistrick (1978).

The height of the droving trade also corresponded with the establishment of the turnpikes, which in some cases took over and improved roads which had long been used for droving. Many of the drovers used these improved roads, as they made rapid and efficient movement possible, even though other users of the turnpikes might be held up. On the other hand, drovers who wished to avoid the toll charges (which could amount to a substantial sum, given the frequency of toll bars and the long distances over which animals were driven) had to find new routes, or ways around the tollgates. As a result, some later drove roads took very peculiar and difficult routes and many drove roads had a network largely independent of the turnpikes.

Drove roads were formerly very numerous, though now their physical remains tend to be rather fragmentary, giving little idea of the original network, especially in lowland England. They can

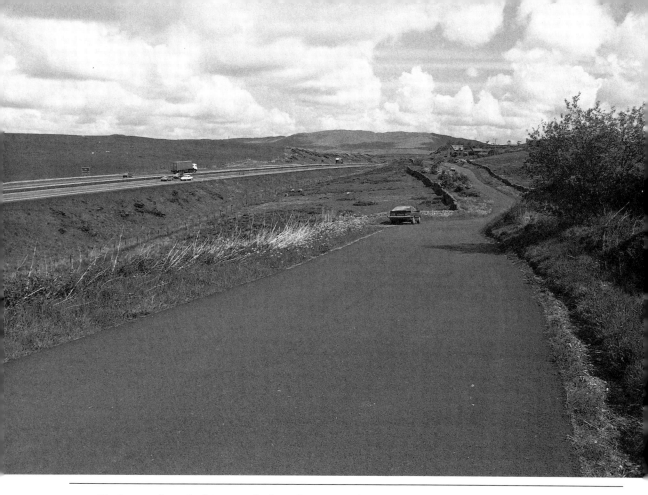

42 *Cattle were formerly driven south along this section of Galwaithegate, until the railway over Shap was completed in 1846; the M6 now carries most of the traffic.*

appear in very different forms – they may be wide swathes across open hill or moorland where there was little to stop the animals choosing their own course, or narrow sunken roads (holloways) where there was a steep slope or some other constriction, or again wide enclosed lanes running through farmland. Some drove roads are now overlain by modern highways, but many others survive as country lanes. Yet others have been lost through disuse, or, especially in Wales, destroyed by recent afforestation. Most drove roads were punctuated by overnight grazing grounds (stances or halts); they were typically 8 to 12 miles (12 to 20km) apart, and often had an inn. These roads were not used solely by drovers, but by a great variety of travellers.

Drove roads can be traced in a variety of ways; there are the actual remains of the tracks, written records of the trade itself, descriptions written by contemporary travellers and maps or road books naming certain roads as droves. Even inn, farm, road and place names can give useful clues: field names such as Half Penny Field may relate to overnight stopping places, and inn names along drove roads include Drover's Rest, Black Bull, White Ox or Brown Cow. In England, the inn names may refer to the origins of the droves, such as Scotch Inn, Welsh Arms or Craven Heifer, with more unusual examples including Tam O'Shanter, Highland Laddie and Caledonian. Because many inns have ceased to trade, and others changed their names

43 *One of the many drove routes out of the Eden valley passed between Wild Boar Fell and Mallerstang Edge; this road above Garsdale Head is still known as Galloway Gate. In the hey-day of droving there were no walls and probably no precisely defined track.*

since droving ended, it is better to check lists of inns in early nineteenth-century directories. The antiquity of droving is well demonstrated by the road name *Galwaithegate* (the Galloway Road) given to a road south of Tebay in a late twelfth-century charter (Fig. 42). Not far away there is also a track still marked on the OS map as Galloway Gate going south from Mallerstang towards Ribblehead (Fig. 43).

Scottish drove roads

This network extended right up into the Highlands and Islands with a multitude of tracks leading across the hills, aiming for various local cattle markets. There were essentially two main streams: one from the west coast and Skye, and the other from the far north. In the early days, these streams converged on Crieff, where the most important cattle fair or Tryst was held in the early autumn each year until 1770; it was then transferred to Falkirk. Here many of the cattle were bought by English dealers, and driven on southwards. Defoe, writing in 1726, noted that some cattle were driven all the way from Caithness to East Anglia, a distance of around 600 miles (965km). Very few glens in the Highlands or the numerous routes into England did not see the passage of large herds of cattle at some time; though the routes in use at any particular date can be difficult to ascertain (Fig. 44) (Haldane, 1973; Moir, 1975). Moreover, many areas were not farmed and thus not enclosed, and so the drove roads would not have been precisely defined; rather the drovers and their cattle would have taken whatever route seemed easiest, just as had been the case with the prehistoric trackways (see Chapter 2).

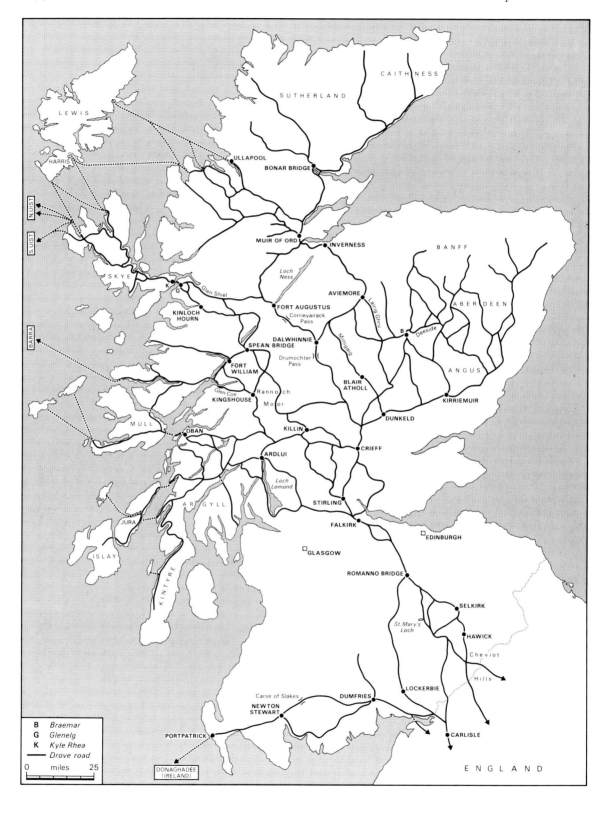

B *Braemar*
G *Glenelg*
K *Kyle Rhea*
── *Drove road*

0   miles   25

44 *The complex network of Scots drove roads extended to the far north and west of the country, but all the routes headed for thr Trysts at Crieff and then Falkirk. (After Haldane, 1973.)*

The Highlands and Islands were suited for little else but the rearing of cattle, and those areas close to the sea with milder climates were especially favoured, even though they were extremely remote from the markets. There were numerous local collecting centres where cattle were gathered together. Beasts from the outer islands were taken to Skye, and then forced to swim across to the mainland at Kyle Rhea, near Glenelg (Fig. 45).

The importance of this trade explains why a barracks was built close by (at Bernera) after the 1715 rising. There was a choice of routes onward; the first was over the Ratagan pass to Glen Shiel and the Great Glen and then over the high Corrieyairack Pass to Crieff, a route which was to be one of the first military roads (see Chapter 7). Another route from Kyle Rhea lay further south, via Kinloch Hourn and Glen Garry to Spean Bridge, a route which Telford proposed making into a road in 1811 (see Chapter 8). From here, there were three possible routes, and most cattle met again at the head of Glencoe before crossing Rannoch Moor (Fig. 46). This is only the barest description of the many routes used

45 *Cattle gathered from the Hebrides swam across from Skye to the mainland at Kyle Rhea, near Glenelg, before starting the long drove south to the markets in England.*

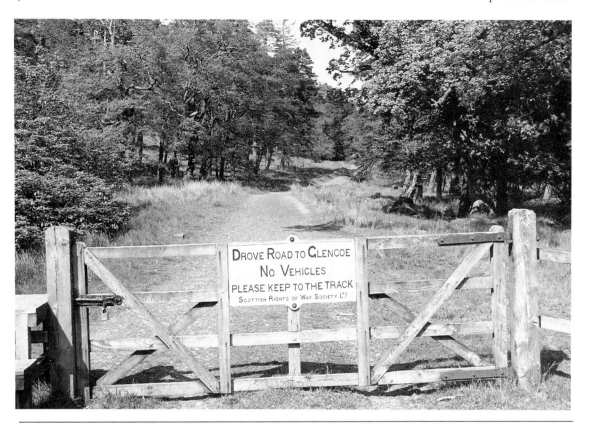

46   *A drove road sign south of the Black Mount is probably incorrect. This is actually the Old Glencoe Road (the Military Road as improved by Telford); the drovers probably went along the other shore of Loch Tulla (see Fig. 71).*

from Skye and the west coast; a host of other routes led in from Arisaig, Mull, Argyll, Islay and Kintyre.

The story is similarly complex for the cattle from the rest of Scotland. The main routes from the north converged on Muir of Ord, and then divided again, one way going via Inverness and Aviemore, the other via Fort Augustus and over the Corrieyairack Pass. The latter was evidently preferred, even though it was a harder route, possibly because the drovers chose to be further away from civilization, but certainly because cheaper and abundant grazing was available. The two routes met again to cross the Drumochter Pass, now followed by the railway and the much improved A9 (Fig. 47).

To the east are two long-disused tracks from Speyside to Blair Atholl; the older is Comyn's Road which was built in the thirteenth century, and was later known as the Way of the Waggon Wheels. It was replaced by the Minigaig Pass even further east in the sixteenth century. Both routes were shorter than Drumochter, but both climbed much higher (reaching 790 and 836m (2600 and 2745ft) respectively (Kerr, 1991; Storer, 1991). They were replaced by the military road over Drumochter in 1729. Many other Highland drove routes were followed by the eighteenth-century military roads (see Chapter 7), whilst others were improved in the early nineteenth century by Telford, who was much concerned to help

47 *The Drumochter Pass is now traversed by the A9, leaving little trace of the drovers who once passed this way from the north of Scotland towards the Trysts.*

the droving trade (see Chapter 8).

Moray, Aberdeen and Angus had their own rather less rugged routes to the Trysts, long before this part of Scotland became famous for cattle breeding. In these lower coastal areas, many old drove roads have disappeared beneath later roads, been compressed between walls, or been obliterated by enclosure or new fields.

South of Falkirk, several routes led over the hills towards England. The routes spread out as there was no immediate common goal, and there are several relatively easy alternative routes. Most cattle seem to have been driven across the Pentland Hills via Cauldstane Slap to Romanno Bridge. One route then went down the Annan valley to Lockerbie and Carlisle, whilst others went via Selkirk and Hawick either to Teviothead, Langholm and Carlisle or into the Tyne valley along the Roman Dere Street, heading for the Great North Road and eastern England. Many early maps of this area depict drove roads across the southern uplands and the Cheviots. Much of this area was devoid of settlement and agriculture, and presented few obstructions to the drovers.

The only area of southern Scotland which produced cattle for the droving trade was Galloway, and in addition cattle were brought across from Ireland to Portpatrick. All these cattle were driven eastwards to Dumfries, and then either joined the Scots cattle at Carlisle, or were driven across the sands of the Solway Firth into Cumberland;

48   *Scots cattle were driven across the border along numerous routes, heading south for the growing towns of England; many stopped along the way to be fattened. (After Bonser, 1970.)*

these sands routes became more frequented after the roads around Carlisle were turnpiked, despite the obvious dangers (see Chapter 7). There were several different routes across the sands, but the westernmost, from Dornoch to Bowness, led to the cattle-fair ground at Rosley, exactly a day's drive to the south. Here they were joined by cattle bred or fattened on the English side of the Solway, before moving on to Penrith, and perhaps to the important fair at Brough.

By the middle of the eighteenth century, a large proportion of the 80,000 cattle crossing the border each year passed through Cumberland (Fig. 48). Beyond Penrith and Brough the routes spread out again, leading into Westmorland, Lancashire and Yorkshire, usually keeping to the higher ground. Many of these survive as the green roads of the Pennines which provide numerous grand walking routes (Raistrick, 1978). Some cattle were fattened in Craven, as they were now only a short distance from the rapidly growing industrial towns of northern England. The cattle destined for East Anglia and London generally headed for the Great North Road, with Boroughbridge and Wetherby being the most important meeting points; up to

30,000 cattle passed through Wetherby each year in the 1770s, with up to 2000 a day in the busy season.

The Hambleton drove road deserves a special mention as it is one of the best preserved lengths still to be seen in England. It is part of the route from Durham to York and passes over the western end of the Cleveland Hills, reaching a height of 385m (1257ft). It is a classic example of the drovers' use of a hill track rather than the turnpiked road in the vale below (Fig. 49). The road is also known locally as the Thieves' Highway, and the Coach Road, though its rough surface was never fit for wheeled traffic. The road leaves the lower ground at Swainby, and climbs through Scarth Nick on to the long ridge of the Hambleton Hills; the climb to the summit of Black Hambleton is heavily eroded, but the 6 miles (10km) from there to Sneck Yate has probably changed little since the drovers' time.

This section is now part of the Cleveland Way long-distance footpath. The drove road goes for about 15 miles (24km) to the top of Sutton Bank, where it divides for York and Malton. There were once four inns along the way, each providing overnight grazing and other comforts. The first, the Chequers Inn, still stands, though it is now a farmhouse; only the Hambleton Hotel is still in business, serving travellers on the busy A170 at the top of Sutton Bank.

Further south the cattle drovers used a variety of routes, often preferring old tracks which kept to higher ground, avoided villages or which had not been turnpiked. Sections of the Old North Road were used, as was the Roman road south of Lincoln (Ermine Street or High Dyke; see Fig. 28). Sewstern Lane from Newark joins Ermine Street just north of Stamford; it is often quoted as a prehistoric route, but was still used by the drovers, from whom it acquired its alternative name of The Drift.

Many Scots cattle were diverted from the

49   The drove road over Black Hambleton is clearly shown on Jefferys' map of Yorkshire (1771). (Reproduced by courtesy of H. Margary.)

trek southwards to be driven into East Anglia for fattening. Various routes were taken through Lincolnshire, often crossing the Trent at Gainsborough. Most cattle entered Norfolk at Wisbech, heading for St Faith's Fair, north of Norwich. The importance of this trade is attested by the villages which have the word Drove in their names (such as Whaplode Drove and Holbeach Drove). The cattle were eventually driven to London's Smithfield Market, sometimes along ancient tracks such as the Peddars Way and Icknield Way, or along newer roads such as that through Sudbury and Chelmsford. A peculiarity in East Anglia was that geese and turkeys were also driven to London.

Welsh drove roads

The Welsh droving trade was in most respects very similar to that in Scotland, but the most important difference was that sheep were also driven. Less research has been undertaken than in Scotland, and the known network of drove roads in Wales is still incomplete, especially in the north of the country, though there are several recent useful studies (Godwin & Toulson, 1977; Colyer, 1976 and 1984). One type of evidence which is more useful here than in Scotland is the nineteenth-century cartographic record. There are various large-scale county maps dating from 1785 to 1830, and the Ordnance Survey one-inch

was published between 1818 and 1841, followed by the 6-inch from 1860 to 1888. There are also the tithe maps of the period around the 1840s. All these maps depict the roads at a time when droving was still active, or very soon after. Place names are also useful: *ffordd, heol* and *sarn* mean road, *rhyd* is a ford and *sais* means English, no doubt often referring to the cattle dealers.

Cattle rearing became a vital part of the Welsh economy, and the tentacles of the network of drove roads spread out to the far west of Wales. There is a Drovers' Arms as far west as Newcastle Emlyn, and there are many others in remote corners of the Welsh hills, originally well placed to serve the drovers. The roads do not head for a single

50   *The drove roads from the southern part of west Wales took a variety of routes into England. (After Colyer, 1976.)*

51 *Welsh drove roads across the English Midlands; most headed towards London. (After Bonser, 1970; Colyer, 1976.)*

market, as in Scotland, but converge into one of the several routes into England (Fig. 50). The northern drove routes start out in Anglesey, the Lleyn Peninsula, or around Harlech, and go round Snowdonia, across high wastelands and peat bogs towards Ruthin for northern England, or Shrewsbury for the Midlands and South.

From central Wales, cattle and sheep were driven from Machynlleth and Mallwyd over the hills or along the turnpikes towards Welshpool and Shrewsbury, or further south over the Kerry Ridgeway, which begins at the Cider House where the drovers

could obtain refreshment. This route crosses Offa's Dyke before descending to Bishop's Castle, and then proceeds to Plowden where the drovers usually climbed on to the even bigger ridge of The Long Mynd. As already mentioned, both these ridge routes probably have prehistoric origins. Other cattle from west mid-Wales were gathered at centres such as Llanddewibrefi, Tregaron, Ffair Rhos or Cwmystwyth, before crossing the hills towards Kington and Leominster. One of the most important routes led from Tregaron to Abergwesyn (now a metalled road) and Beulah.

Further south again, animals were driven from the area around Lampeter and the Teifi valley to the village of Caeo, which hosted one of the largest cattle fairs in this part of Wales. From there, cattle might go from Tafarn Talgarth and Llanddulas over the Epynt hills; this track is another of the more famous drove roads (Colyer, 1984). It traverses remote hills at up to 460m (1500ft) in height, though the drove road is now lost amongst the more recent tracks made for army purposes, and attempting to trace it is not advised. The route crosses the present B4519 at the old Drovers' Arms and then descends to ford the Wye north of Erwood, before climbing again to Painscastle and back down to the river at Rhydyspence, where the drovers joined the turnpike to Hereford. Cattle from Pembrokeshire and Carmarthen might have proceeded via Trecastle to Brecon. From there they might

have gone north to the Wye valley, or south to Monmouth, perhaps being ferried across the Severn north of Bristol for sale in the south-west of England.

A great variety of routes then led on towards the towns of central and southern England (Fig. 51). From north Wales, the cattle would travel via Wrexham, Whitchurch and Newport to join Watling Street. From Shrewsbury the usual route went along Watling Street (now the A5) as far as High Cross, where the drovers turned off through Lutterworth for the important market at Northampton. From here, some cattle were driven to East Anglia for fattening.

Further south another route, known as the Welsh Road, left Watling Street at Brownhills and went via Sutton Coldfield, Kenilworth and Southam for Buckingham. Many parts of this country road have the

54 *Banbury Lane, heading towards Northampton, is alternately a minor road and green lane as it passes through the more recent enclosed fields.*

52 and 53 *(Left and above)   The Welsh Road passing through Warwickshire avoids many of the villages. In Southam, many miles from the Welsh border, the memory of the drovers survives in the road name.*

typical features of a drove road, especially beyond Kenilworth. It has wide grass verges for grazing and it tends to go past rather than through villages (rather unusual in a country lane), there are also sundry field and place names referring to both Wales and London; in many places it is still called Welsh Road (Figs. 52 and 53). It has survived because it was never turnpiked, unlike the parallel A5. From Buckingham, two routes led on, one to rejoin Watling Street at Dunstable, the other to Aylesbury and Wendover.

Cattle coming out of Wales through Leominster or Hereford also used a variety of routes. Those destined for East Anglia might head across the Cotswolds for Banbury, from where the ancient Banbury Lane leads to Northampton, crossing the Welsh Road at Culworth. This lane is now the B4525 to Thorpe Mandeville, and then becomes a wide minor road or green lane passing through later enclosures (Fig. 54). Cattle from Hereford and Monmouth heading for London might take a more southerly route, perhaps via Gloucester, Burford, Thame and Amersham, or via Gloucester and Cricklade, heading for the easy going of the prehistoric Berkshire Ridgeway at Liddington. In between these routes was another route, part of which, from north of Cirencester to Lechlade, was known as the Welsh Way. Like so many of these routes, it wound its way across the country, often keeping to higher ground and avoiding the turnpikes and their tollgates. Some cattle driven along these routes were destined to go straight to the London markets, but many went to be fattened in Essex and Kent.

The widespread nature of this trade can be seen from the fact that the former Drovers' Inn in Stockbridge (Hampshire), many miles from the Welsh border, still has a sign written in Welsh offering good hay, pasture, beer and bed. This was a stopping place for drovers on their way to Portsmouth.

Many parts of England have local drovers' routes. In Derbyshire, for example, such a road ran from Congleton across the hills above Leek to Hartington and Winster, heading for Nottingham. On the way there is still an Oxhay Farm, and the former drovers' inn near Oxbatch is now the Mermaid Inn (Dodd, 1980). In Cumbria, there are several local drove roads along the west coast, leading first to local fairs such as those at Boonwood or Arlecdon, and then either straight across the passes to Ambleside, or around the northern edge of the hills to Cockermouth and Rosley, in both cases so that local cattle could join the main droves of Scots cattle southwards.

The routes described above are only a few of the routes which were available, and it is clear that the precise routes used would depend on numerous factors including the drovers' personal preference, tradition, increasing congestion, deteriorating accommodation for man or beast, the weather, the creation of new enclosures or turnpikes, or the erection of new tollgates.

Droving reached its peak in the 1830s, but ceased during the second half of the nineteenth century as the railways progressively reached out towards the north and west of Britain. Often the droves would disappear almost overnight as the cattle were transferred to the trains, leaving the drove roads empty of cattle, and the droving inns and stances without trade. The first drove roads to cease to be used as such were those nearest to London, as cattle were driven only as far as the new railheads. The pattern of droving changed as the railway network

grew; a curious example is that Welsh cattle were driven *to* Aberystwyth once the railway there was opened, completely reversing the previous direction of droving. The last cattle drove right across Wales took place in 1870, though shorter droves lingered on into the twentieth century until cattle trucks running on metalled roads finally rendered even the short droves to the railhead unnecessary.

In Scotland another factor in the decline of drove roads was that cattle were beginning to be moved by steamship around the coast from the 1830s, but the railways had a great impact here too. The last drove over the Corrieyairack Pass was probably in 1906, but by then the whole Scottish droving trade had long been in decline, the Falkirk Tryst had already ceased, as both cattle and sheep sped southwards with ease on the new iron roads.

Many drove roads have been little used since the mid-nineteenth century, except by walkers and horse riders but many remain in a good physical condition. Their continuing legal status as byways means that it is perfectly legal to drive vehicles along them (see Chapter 10) and the increasing number of motorbikes and four-wheel drive vehicles in the hands of people with no respect for the countryside is becoming a problem in some areas. It needs only a few thoughtless drivers to churn up a green road, making it anything but a pleasure for more traditional travellers. Often local by-laws can solve the problem, but if the problem gets worse, a change in the law regarding rights of way may be needed in order to preserve these old tracks.

Packhorse tracks

Before the improvement of the roads in the eighteenth century, which allowed wheeled vehicles to reach all the major centres of population, most goods had to be carried by packhorse (Hey, 1980). This was true throughout England, but especially so in the more hilly areas such as the Pennines and the Lake District, as well as in much of Wales and Scotland. Thus the packhorse train was a common sight on all roads until they were improved by the turnpikes, and made fit for wagon and coach traffic.

In the Lake District, it was impossible to get any vehicle wider than a horse westwards from Kendal until after 1750. From Kendal, gangs of horses travelled not only to numerous places in and around the Lake District, but also to destinations including Glasgow, Barnard Castle, York, Leeds, Hull, Wigan, Manchester, Liverpool, Norwich and London. Packhorses were a flexible and reliable means of transport, able to carry up to about 150kg (3cwt) each. But they were rather slow, making perhaps only 15 miles (24km) a day in hilly country, though about 25 miles (40km) a day was probably a better average. This meant that the journey from Kendal to London took up to two weeks, and that from Exeter to London took a week. If perishable goods such as fish had to be sent a long distance, then changes of horses might be used, allowing 60 miles (95km) a day or more to be achieved. Defoe noted that fresh salmon were being sent from Workington to London in the 1720s:

this is performed with horses, which, changing often, go Night and Day without intermission, and, . . . very much out-go the Post.

Given the poor condition and narrowness of most roads, packhorses were faster and more reliable than carts until the roads were improved. It is important to remember that the Industrial Revolution had its origins in the packhorse era, and this was certainly true for the textile industries on either side of the Pennines; many of the first mills, which were sited in the hills to take advantage of water power, could only receive and despatch goods by horse for many years.

These tracks are often referred to 'pack and prime ways' or as 'causeys', and were maintained by the parish. As with drovers' roads, inn names such as Pack Horse, Bay Horse, String of Horses and Woolpack can give useful clues to the former presence of a packhorse route in both town and country. Packhorse tracks were not usually engineered or metalled, except where conditions were difficult, such as across boggy ground or steep slopes; at best they were only roughly paved. Steep slopes were often overcome by the use of zigzags, which may have survived either because the later improved routes were unable to follow their gradients and sharp bends, or because such routes have not been replaced at all, and remain in use as footpaths. In general, few of these old narrow tracks still survive, as most have been widened for wheeled traffic.

A frequent surviving feature of the

55 *Slater's Bridge in Little Langdale was probably built around 1700, and is typical of the many Lakeland packhorse bridges which formed a crucial part of the network of tracks through the fells.*

packhorse trade is the packhorse bridge. They were built because it was unsafe to drive a heavily laden horse with a valuable load across a stream of any depth. They are easily recognizable, being narrow and having low parapets (or none at all) to accommodate the loads slung on each side of the horses; parapets were sometimes added later. There are many examples throughout the country. They are occasionally referred to locally as 'Roman' bridges, but the earliest are medieval. Those in the Lake District seem to have been built in the years around 1700, coinciding with a great growth in trading (Fig. 55). A few, such as Stockley Bridge in Borrowdale and the Doctor's Bridge in Eskdale, have been widened to allow other traffic to use them.

The mountain passes of the Lake District which have escaped being made into motor roads show what many of the packhorse tracks were once like. Virtually every Lakeland mountain pass has an old narrow track, usually with zigzags in the steeper portions (Hindle, 1984). The track from Wasdale Head over Sty Head Pass to Borrowdale is a good example; the County Council was still maintaining part of it in 1930, and sections have recently been rebuilt. From Wasdale Head, the old track keeps close to the beck, unlike the modern direct but stony path which slopes up beneath Great Gable. The old track then crosses Spouthead Gill, and ascends in a fine series of zigzags, mostly still with grass underfoot, eventually rejoining the later path at the top of the pass (Fig. 56).

Another good example is the Stake Pass from Langdale to Borrowdale. The zigzags on the Langdale side have recently been

---

56 *Many of the mountain tracks in the Lake District are little changed from the days of the packhorses; in particular most of the old passes have well-made zigzag paths.*

brought back into use; they provide clear evidence that this route was actually engineered, though by whom and at what date is impossible to determine. West's *Guide to the Lakes* of 1780 describes the pass as:

an Alpine journey . . . The road makes many traverses so close, that at every flexure it seems almost to return into itself, and such as are advancing in different traverses, appear to go different ways.

Further east, Grisedale Hause, from Grasmere to Ullswater, is still described on the OS map as an 'Old Packhorse Road', while the north side of Gatescarth Pass, ascending from Mardale, has another fine set of zigzags, which were once improved to allow coaches to pass. An example of a packhorse track which was improved is the route from Kendal towards Ulverston; it was turnpiked in 1763. There are still 16 steep hills between Kendal and Newby Bridge, and the worst, at Strawberry Bank, has a sharp steep zigzag, but at least it also has a pub half way up.

There are many packhorse tracks in the Pennines, and the area around Haslingden and Todmorden is particularly rich, with numerous tracks climbing and criss-crossing the hills, mostly at a height of between 150 and 300m (500 and 1000ft) (Fig. 57). Many survive as lines of stones about 60cm (24in) wide, running across fields, and even across open moorland. Essentially they form a network of tracks related to the scattered upland industrial sites of the late eighteenth century. They also neatly avoided the turnpikes which were built later along the valley bottoms. As most are on higher ground, and were of little interest to the later industrial developments in the valleys, they have not been incorporated into the modern road system, and many have survived.

One of the best known is the Reddyshore Scoutgate (roughly meaning 'steep red hill road') which clings to a shelf some 90m

57   *There are numerous packhorse tracks running around the Pennine valleys, keeping between the valley bottoms and the often misty higher ground.*

(300ft) above the western side of the gap through the Pennines from Littleborough to Todmorden; this causey is paved with large stone flags for much of its length (Fig. 58). Going north past a stone guide post, the track descends into the valley, but immediately climbs the eastern slope, heading for Lumbutts. This section is known as Saltersrake Gate (i.e. a possible saltway). Beyond Lumbutts, the track continues towards Cragg Vale and still

58   *The Reddyshore Scoutgate is a classic example of a Pennine packhorse track, keeping high above the floor of the valley.*

59 and 60 *Above the old industrial village of Lumbutts (near Todmorden) the single line of paving leads between walls, and then on to the moor towards Stoodley Pike.*

survives in an excellent state of preservation (Figs. 59 and 60).

Another example of a road named after a specific commodity is the Limersgate from Burnley to Rochdale. Lime was carried along it to help improve the poor soils of the south Pennines, and to be used in the building trade; coal was carried on the return journey north. It is slightly unusual in reaching a height of over 425m (1400ft), as such routes usually avoided the misty conditions which might be encountered above 300m (1000ft). The northern section is now a motor road (A671), but south of Thieveley Pike the track follows the ridge across the open moorland to Rochdale and is largely overgrown, with little of the original stonework to be seen.

Another well-known track in this area is The Long Causeway which runs across the moors from Burnley to Halifax. It is probably of great antiquity. It was certainly used in the Middle Ages by the monks of Whalley Abbey, and was formerly marked by several wayside crosses. It is now a metalled road for most of its length, and the central section, from Mere Clough to Hebden Bridge makes a pleasant alternative to the modern A646 in the valleys below. Only on Stiperden Moor does the modern road divert from the old route for a mile to avoid descending to a stream.

In most upland areas of Britain, there are many tracks leading from the farms and villages, giving access to the moors for grazing, turbary (peat cutting), quarrying or mining; they are often referred to as accommodation roads (see Chapter 9). On Dartmoor, many of these tracks have become deeply etched in the landscape, some of which bear names such as Black

Lane or Blackwood Path, a reference to the carriage of peat. The remote routes across Dartmoor were first marked by stone crosses, and later by wayside stones or even signposts, many of which still survive.

Certain tracks seem to have become associated with the carriage of specific commodities – Limersgate has already been mentioned – and other goods which have given their names to roads include wool, coal, iron, lead, charcoal and peat. However the most famous connections are with salt and corpses (see Chapter 7 and 4 respectively).

Reconstructing the network of these tracks is vital to the understanding of the economic system of the sixteenth to the eighteenth centuries. The packhorse system reached its peak during the eighteenth century, but the creation of turnpikes gradually provided a much better alternative means of transport, even in remote areas. Many packhorse tracks fell into disuse, some disappearing entirely from the map, though others continued to be used, and remain as tracks or roads today.

7 Unusual roads

Several unusual types of roads deserve a chapter to themselves. There are those such as sands routes and early industrial routes which do not fit neatly into the chronological history of most roads around which this book is structured. There are also the military roads which were built for political reasons, rather than for the simple economic need for new roads. All these roads are limited in number and are found only in particular areas.

Sands routes

In certain parts of Britain, travellers commonly left *terra firma* and travelled across bays and estuaries, usually to save the time which the much longer road journey would entail. Cattle were also driven across sands routes, thus avoiding paying turnpike tolls; the use of the fords across the Solway has already been mentioned (Chapter 6). In Northumberland the sands and the links

61 *Routes across the Lavan Sands to Anglesey as shown on Evans' map of 1795.*

62 *The milestone in the centre of Cartmel gives the distances across the sands as a matter of course. The modern road distances are 25 and 11 miles (40 and 18km) respectively.*

behind them were used as the easiest way along the coast, whilst in North Wales the usual route to Anglesey was from Penmaen or Aber across the Lavan Sands to Beaumaris, rather than going to the ferry at Bangor; both routes are clearly shown on Evans' map of 1795 (Fig. 61).

The best known of routes 'over-the-sands' were those across Morecambe Bay, leading from Lancaster to the Cartmel and Furness peninsulas (Fig. 62) (Hindle, 1984). These routes have been in use for hundreds of years, and were certainly well used in the Middle Ages. The three local monastic houses were probably the first to appoint guides, and two are still appointed today (one each for the Kent and Leven crossings).

The reason for the popularity of this route is obvious: the distance from Lancaster to Ulverston along the old winding and hilly packhorse route via Kendal (turnpiked in 1763) is 41 miles (66km); across the sands it is a flat if damp 19 miles (30.5km). West's *Guide to the Lakes* (1780) describes the crossing as safe and routine, adding that

On a fine day there is not a more pleasant seaside journey in the kingdom.

Indeed, regular coach services began in

1781. But not everyone found the route satisfactory; John Wesley passed this way in 1759, and he was clearly little enamoured of the route:

I have taken my leave of the sand road . . . there are four sands to cross, so far from each other, that it is scarce possible to pass them all in a day: Especially as you have all the way to do with a generation of liars, who detain all strangers as long as they can, either for their own gain or their neighbours. I can advise no stranger to go this way: He may go round by Kendal and Keswick, often in less time, always with less expense, and far less trial of his patience.

But Wesley was travelling all the way to Whitehaven, and crossed not only the estuaries of the Kent and Leven, but also those of the Duddon and Esk. A list of writers who wrote about their crossings includes George Fox, Robert Southey, Thomas De Quincey, William Wordsworth and Mrs Gaskell; J.M.W. Turner also travelled across the sands, leaving several sketches and paintings.

The precise routes taken across the sands obviously changed, as did the channels of the rivers themselves (Fig. 63). From Lancaster, traffic took to the Leven sands at Hest Bank for the 8 miles (13km) across to the Cartmel peninsula at Kent's Bank (Fig. 64). Here most travellers would stop at the small town of Flookburgh for refreshment. There were then three alternative routes across the often more treacherous Leven sands to reach Ulverston and the Furness peninsula. The crossings of the Duddon and Esk estuaries were usually much easier.

Even the building of a new slightly shorter turnpike via Levens Bridge in 1818 (now the A590) did little to diminish the sands traffic. The sands route still had the advantage of being toll-free, though crossing times were of course determined by the tides. It was not until the railway from Carnforth to Ulverston and the new town of Barrow was completed in 1857 that the traffic across the sands finally ceased.

63   *Routes across the Kent and Leven estuaries of Morecambe Bay which took travellers to the Cartmel and Furness peninsulas until the coastal railway was opened in 1857. The river channels are shown as on the first edition one-inch maps.*

Early industrial roads

Since medieval times, certain routes have been associated with the carriage of specific commodities and the most famous are the so-called 'saltways'. Salt was needed everywhere, but was found in only a few localities; the main sources were in the wiches of Cheshire (Northwich, Middlewich, Nantwich) and Droitwich,

64 *Travellers crossing the Kent sands came ashore near Grange, and climbed Cart(er) Lane before crossing the Cartmel peninsula (see Fig. 63).*

plus various saltings around the coast. From each a variety of routes spread outwards. They are known from documentary evidence as early as the late Saxon period, though the trade was certainly carried on long before.

On the ground these routes can often be traced by 'salt' place-names. The 'saltway' from Northwich to Sheffield goes via Macclesfield and Chapel-en-le-Frith, passing Salter's Knowl, Salter Barn, Saltergate Lane and even a Psalter Lane (formerly without the P) on the way. It is, however, rather dubious to try to concoct a 'saltway' route based only on a few far flung place-names. Another danger in calling a track a saltway is that it gives the impression that nothing else was ever carried along it; in fact, these tracks were just ordinary roads or packhorse routes, along which salt was commonly carried. Most were only occasionally referred to as 'salt' routes when the trade was at its height.

Equally, references are sometimes seen to 'wool packroads' and the like. Such names are often derived from flimsy evidence, the roads were rarely given such names in the past, and again they give the false notion that only the one commodity was carried. On all these grounds such misleading oversimplified descriptions should be avoided. The most peculiar example known to the author is the suggestion that there were two 'snuff packroads' from Whitehaven to Penrith and to Kendal; here the matter is made worse in that the commodity being transported was not snuff at all, but tobacco.

Nevertheless, there are historically identifiable routes of this kind, for example the Jobbers' Roads around and across Dartmoor have received detailed attention (Hemery, 1986). The best known ran the 12 miles (20km) from Sheepstor to Buckfastleigh, and wool was carried along it from the farms and villages *en route* to be woven; it has been erroneously called the Abbot's Way (see Chapter 4). Place-names should always be interpreted with great care, for their meanings are not always obvious, and the names of roads also change over time. The medieval Wool Street (the Roman *Via Devana* south-east of Cambridge) in fact got its name from wolves rather than from wool. The publications of the English Place-Name Society should always be consulted.

Among the earliest industrial routes are the tracks leading to the numerous quarries which are scattered all over Britain. These roads were often nothing more than self-made local tracks, yet they had to be kept in a reasonable state of repair, as the stone was usually transported by cart or wagon. If a long journey was in prospect, it was taken by boat as much as possible; the famous quarries at Barnack, near Stamford, were well-served by the river systems draining into the Wash.

More remote quarries required new roads to be built, and the quarries at Honister Pass in the Lake District provide an excellent example of the difficulties which had to be overcome (see Fig. 56). The best slates are found above the top of the pass, at some

610m (2000ft) above sea level where mining began in 1643. The nearest seaport was at Drigg, some 14 miles (22km) to the south-west, but Great Gable provided an immediate obstacle. It has long been claimed that the slate was loaded on to wooden sleds, and pulled around Gable on a track ('sledgate') which became known as Moses Trod. This route is generally level, but has a steep climb into the gap between Gable and Kirk Fell, before dropping steeply down to Wasdale Head. The slate was then supposedly sent down the lake by boat, leaving only a few miles overland to the coast.

It seems very unlikely, however, that sleds could have been operated successfully over the very rough ground of the fells; it would have been difficult to move a loaded sled on the level, and impossible up a slope. Thus the use of this route by sleds is extremely doubtful. It is much more likely that the slate was always taken down either side of Honister Pass; indeed in the nineteenth century the quarry company built a road down to Seatoller in Borrowdale, and charged tolls for anyone else who wished to use it. This road has not been surfaced with tarmac, and can still be followed as an easier alternative (Fig. 65 and see Fig. 56) (Hindle, 1984).

In the Furness peninsula, the Burlington slate quarries high on the hill above Sand Side used to send their slates to be loaded on to vessels beached in the Duddon estuary below. However, when the Ulverston Canal was opened in 1796, a specially constructed 'slate road' was built to take

65 *The well-graded Honister quarry road (on the left) became a toll road for the early tourists; the modern tarmaced road is much steeper (see Fig. 56).*

advantage of the new port and the bigger ships which could berth there, even though a much longer road journey was involved. There are also numerous quarrymen's paths around Dartmoor (Hemery, 1986).

Early mining activity also had associated routeways, whatever mineral was being mined. Thus there are tracks leading from Yorkshire coal, Derbyshire lead and Cornish tin mines, to name but three. Some of the tinners' roads are dealt with by Toulson (1984). Often named roads give a clue to long-abandoned workings. In the Yorkshire Dales, at the head of Dentdale, the OS map still shows a 'Coal Road' leading to various disused coal pits high on the fells. Curiously, the upper part of this road is the drove road named 'Galloway Gate' (see Chapter 6). A few miles to the south, near Ingleton, there is a 'Turbary Road' above Kingsdale, which once gave access to the local peat cuttings.

With the growth of industry, however, especially from the mid-eighteenth century, improved methods of transport were required. On the larger scale, this led to the three successive manias of turnpike, canal and railway building, but locally, individual entrepreneurs built their own roads to serve their factories and mines. Although usually quite short, many of these roads have now become part of the public road system, especially where the industry or mine they once served has long since disappeared.

The canal mania led to the construction of about 4000 miles (6400km) of canals, virtually all with towpaths for the horses which originally provided the locomotive power. Although these paths were originally intended solely for the use of the canal companies, they have now become valuable recreational routes. Many canal tunnels had no towpath, and narrow horse tracks had to be built over the hills. An example is the sunken Boat Lane leading over the Pennines from the western portal of the Standedge Tunnel at Diggle (Fig. 96),

while another leads over the much shorter Hincaster Tunnel on the Lancaster canal south of Kendal. Originally the boats had to be legged through the tunnels.

The study of the changes in urban and industrial road systems, especially since about 1800, has barely begun, yet there is no shortage of evidence, whether in documentary or map form. The most obvious cartographic source lies in the early large-scale Ordnance Survey maps, especially where there have been drastic changes in the last 150 years. The first such maps are the 6-inch maps for Lancashire and Yorkshire, surveyed from 1841 to 1854, followed by maps at both 6-inch and 25-inch for all of England and Wales from 1854, completed in 1893, with many subsequent revisions (Hindle, 1988). The many earlier maps, usually at smaller scales, can also be of great use.

Military roads

The most important group of military roads was built in the Scottish highlands in the eighteenth century as a result of Jacobite unrest. In particular the risings of 1715 and 1745 forced the government in London to try to disarm and control the highlanders. In 1724, Major-General Wade was sent to investigate the problem, and his report proposed new companies of soldiers and new forts. He also noted the difficulty of simply getting around the Highlands because of the poor state of the roads and bridges. Wade was rapidly appointed Commander-in-Chief, North Britain, and took up his post in 1725. He began improving communications between the various forts immediately (Taylor, 1976).

The first road to be improved was that along the Great Glen between Fort William and Inverness. Most of it had been completed by 1733, though the High Bridge over the Spean was not completed until

66 *The military roads built by Wade and Caulfeild to help police the Highlands. Wade's original roads simply linked Crieff with the Great Glen, but Caulfeild quadrupled the length of the network. (After Taylor, 1976.)*

1736. By then Wade had overseen the creation of some 250 miles (400km) of military roads, effectively linking the strategic towns of Perth and Stirling with the Great Glen at both Inverness and Fort Augustus (Fig. 66). The roads were as straight as possible, usually 5m (16ft) wide, surfaced with gravel, and their original fords were progressively replaced by bridges.

The road to Inverness included the Corrieyairack Pass which has a series of 11 zigzags on its eastern side (apparently originally 18), and reaches a height of 775m (2543ft) (Figs. 67–70). It is a superbly designed road of which any Roman engineer might have been proud, and was built in only two summer seasons (1731–2). Like many other military roads it followed and improved an existing route, which in this case had been used mainly by drovers (see Chapter 6). It is a very direct route to Fort Augustus, but a curious one in military terms because it must have been blocked by snow for several months each year. Wade reported that it was

now made as easy and practicable for Wheel Carriage as any Road in the country,

but

few travellers agreed, and the rigours of the crossing became legion. Carriages were broken or blown over. Civilians, especially those on foot, died from exposure. (Storer, 1991.)

An unforeseen result of the improvement of the Corrieyairack road was that Bonnie Prince Charlie used it on his way both from

67 *The military road begins its smooth ascent of the eastern side of the Corrieyairack Pass, its surface (and some of its bridges) still in remarkably good condition.*

68 *Eleven well-graded zigzags take the military road to the remote top of the Corrieyairack Pass.*

69 *A magnificent panorama of western Scotland opens up to the west of the Corrieyairack summit (2543ft; 775m).*

70 *A sign at the western end of the Corrieyairack Pass near Fort Augustus records the name of Major-General Wade.*

and back to the Islands in 1745–6. When the road via Loch Laggan was built in 1818 the pass became redundant, and it was not kept in repair after 1830. The bridges were repaired until at least 1850, as the route reverted to being a drove road. The last drove of cattle over the pass took place in 1906, and since then it has become a remote abandoned route, now sadly threatened by four-wheel drive vehicles.

The Scottish military roads as a whole are often referred to as 'Wade's Roads', but in fact about three quarters of them were built under the direction of William Caulfeild (often misspelt), who was appointed Inspector of Roads in 1732, and was largely responsible for building and maintaining all military roads until 1767. Little new construction was undertaken from 1734 until after the 1745 rebellion; but in the following 20 years a further 750 miles

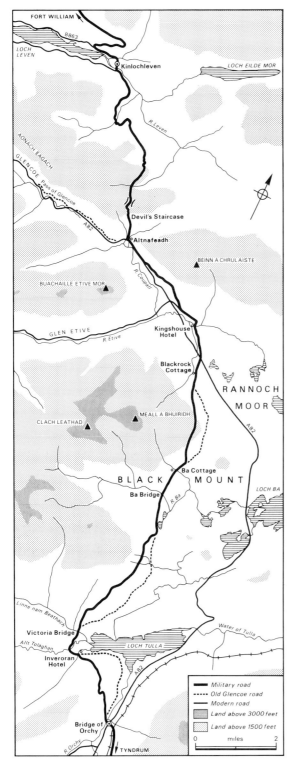

71 *The military and later roads between Bridge of Orchy and Kinlochleven. Drovers had long passed this way before Caulfeild built his road high up to avoid the boggy ground. Certain sections were later improved and the road was rerouted down Glencoe instead of climbing the Devil's Staircase; this second road is now known as the 'Old Glencoe Road'.*

(1200km) of military roads were built. The net result was an integrated network of roads giving three main routes between the Lowlands and the Great Glen as well as numerous interconnecting roads. All this was achieved without the benefit of the new road construction techniques of Telford and McAdam which were to be introduced at the start of the next century.

Perhaps the most famous (or infamous) of Caulfeild's roads are those around Glencoe, which formed part of the route from Stirling to Fort William, built in 1748–53. Most of this road was built alongside the existing drove route. From Bridge of Orchy the original road climbs across the spur of Mam Carraigh, reaching 320m (1050ft), before descending to the Inveroran Hotel (built soon after the road), and then crosses Rannoch Moor well to the west of the present A82, a desolate area known as Black Mount (Fig. 71). Here this original 'Military Road' keeps high in order to avoid boggy ground; in fact it reaches a surprising 500m (1650ft) north of Ba Bridge. Some parts of this road have almost disappeared, whilst others are in reasonable condition. This section ends at Kingshouse, a seventeenth-century inn which was formerly a stance on the drove road and continues to be an important refuge in this remote spot (Fig. 72).

At the head of Glencoe the old road turns to the north, climbing the zigzags of the Devil's Staircase to a height of 550m (1811ft) (Figs. 73 and 74). This is a spectacular ascent, made all the more intriguing as

72 *The military road bridge at the old stance of Kingshouse on Rannoch Moor. The summit of Buachaille Etive Mor is behind.*

Caulfeild could have easily gone round the hill to the east, and avoided the climb entirely! On the staircase modern walkers with no sense of history, and little respect for their leg muscles, have created a new track straight up the hill, largely ignoring the eighteenth-century engineered zigzags. To add insult to the injury already caused to the original road, a totally unnecessary new path across the zigzags has been made.

73 *The Devil's Staircase climbs steeply from Altnafeadh at the western corner of Rannoch Moor, instead of going down Glencoe.*

From the summit the road descends to Kinlochleven, and continues over the pass of Lairig Mhor to Fort William.

Both these passes were abandoned in 1785, when the longer but much easier road through Glencoe was built, leading to the ferry across Loch Leven at Invercoe, and thence around the coast to Fort William. Many other sections of the road were much improved in later years, partly under the direction of Telford, and in particular two new lower alignments were made across Black Mount. The resulting road is rather confusingly called the 'Old Glencoe Road' (see Fig. 46). The long-distance West Highland Way footpath follows it across Rannoch Moor – ignoring the original

74 *The view northwards from the top of the Devil's Staircase is dominated by the Ben Nevis range.*

75 *The Military Road (here the B6318 to the west of Chesters) runs alongside Hadrian's Wall for much of its length. The Wall was partly destroyed when the road was built.*

military road, but then reverting to it across the two passes towards Fort William (Aitken, 1980). The final act in the history of the Glencoe roads was the building of a new motor road from Tyndrum to Ballachulish in the 1930s, leaving most of the earlier roads free of traffic; most are still quite well preserved.

The only completed military road leading to the west of the Great Glen went from Fort Augustus to the barracks at Bernera (built in 1720), which controlled the shortest crossing to Skye (Fig. 66). This first 'Road to the Isles' was built in 1755–63, but it was very difficult to build, and was not maintained after about 1784. When the barracks were abandoned in 1790 it went out of use as there was no economic need for such a remote road. It was not even of much use to the drovers, as their cattle preferred softer ground. It was replaced by the 'Glen Shiel Road' built by Telford early in the nineteenth century; this later road is often at a lower level, and much of it can still be seen

alongside the modern A87 (Fig. 102). What little remains of the military road is more elusive, it is more easily seen on the map than on the ground. Telford's road diverts from the military road at both ends; from Fort Augustus it goes along Loch Ness and into Glen Moriston, avoiding the steep ascent with its six zigzags above the fort. At the western end he built a new road to Kyle of Lochalsh, as well as improving the steep Ratagan Pass to Bernera (see Fig. 103). Curiously, this pass has recently been improved again, even though it is a dead-end road serving only a small population; in the process much of the old road has been destroyed.

By 1800, many of the 1100 miles (1770km) of military roads were in a very poor state as the military need for them had largely vanished, and Parliament was reluctant to put more money into them. However, the social unrest and poor economic conditions in the Highlands prompted the government to ask Telford to build new Highland roads,

---

76 *The central section of the Military Road from Carlisle to Newcastle; built in the 1750s, it follows the Roman Wall, the vallum, or the Stanegate.*

and as part of his work he also improved and maintained over 300 miles (420km) of the military roads in the early years of the nineteenth century (see Chapter 8).

In the south of Scotland a quite separate road was improved to military standards in the 1760s, leading from the English border to Portpatrick, designed to allow English troops to reach the shortest sea-crossing to Ireland without difficulty. It was constructed by improving the existing roads to a width of 5m (16ft), and rebuilding certain bridges. It is now mostly close to or overlain by the A75, except from Annan to Collin and from Dumfries to Castle Douglas where it can be seen in minor roads further south. The major difference from the modern route is between Gatehouse and Creetown where the military road took a more direct route over the Corse of Slakes, a section which sometimes proved impassable in winter. From the start, the Galloway cattle drovers wanted to use this section of the road, but were refused permission; it was replaced by the coastal route by 1790. The road was maintained by the military until 1807.

In addition a military road was built in England, connecting Carlisle and Newcastle, principally because the English troops stationed at Newcastle in 1745 had been unable to cut off the advance of Bonnie Prince Charlie through Carlisle. It was built between 1751 and 1758, and although funded by the government, it operated as a turnpike. Most of its eastern half was built on or close to Hadrian's Wall, and as a result, much of the Wall was used as a cheap and convenient source of stone, and was thus destroyed. This section is now overlain by the A69 from Newcastle to Heddon, and then by the B6318 (Fig. 75). Just before Housesteads a new direct line was laid out, though a short section lies along the vallum of the Wall, and a longer length runs parallel to the Stanegate, which was the Roman frontier road built before the Wall (Fig. 76). From Greenhead the military road is now represented by the A69 again to Brampton, and finally by the B6242 to Carlisle.

8 Turnpikes

The amount of traffic on the major roads of Britain increased fairly steadily from the early sixteenth century, and there was a marked upswing in the years around the start of the eighteenth century. By then the agricultural revolution had already paved the way for the industrial revolution, and the economy, population and towns were all growing rapidly. London was the principal focus of trade, but most other market towns were also growing. Bristol and Norwich were probably the second and third largest towns in 1750, whilst others such as Birmingham, Manchester and Liverpool were not far behind. However, this growth was being restricted by the difficulty of moving goods around the country; there was no incentive to increase production, whether of agricultural or industrial goods, if it was not possible to get the goods to the consumer efficiently, quickly and without raising the price to an unacceptable level.

It is not surprising that the agricultural revolution had begun in East Anglia, or that the first major coal producing and exporting area was Tyneside, as both these areas had relatively easy sea-borne access to London. Since medieval times rivers had been used to transport heavy and bulky goods, as the cost of sending goods by water was only a fraction of the cost by road, and some roads acted as feeders to the various ports. But the river and coastal shipping systems had their natural limitations: some areas were remote from navigable water, whilst elsewhere

rivers ran in the wrong direction. Many areas remote from river or sea transport had great difficulty in getting their agricultural or industrial goods to market. In any case, certain types of traffic were unsuited to carriage by water; for example, it was much easier and cheaper to drive animals overland to market (see Chapter 6). Overall, most roads were used quite independently of water transport.

The roads had not seen any deliberate skilled engineering or construction since Roman times, but were being repaired on an *ad hoc* basis, by labour from each parish through which they passed, under the system established in 1555 (Chapter 5). It became increasingly difficult for certain parishes to maintain their roads, especially if a particularly busy route ran through. Some parishes were reluctant to undertake their statutory duties, some were too small and poor, whilst others were simply incompetent. There was no national planning of road repairs; any incentive for repairs, let alone improvements, had to come from interested local people. Only in a handful of places did individual landowners undertake any private repairing of roads. In order to try to alleviate the growing problems, Parliament took various steps from 1621, including limiting the weight of vehicles and banning narrow wheels in an attempt to reduce damage to the roads. An act of 1691 distinguished clearly between 'drift ways' (for foot and horse traffic only) and 'cartways'; even in this act their respective widths were required to be only 3 and 8 feet.

The idea of charging tolls in order to finance road improvements (effectively privatizing roads) was put forward several times during the seventeenth century, but was resisted. The simple notion that road users should pay for the upkeep of roads in relation to the damage which they caused was for many years too revolutionary for Parliament to contemplate. Some idea of the problems may be gained from a bill presented in 1621–2, which proposed to charge tolls to repair the Old Great North Road between Biggleswade and Baldock. It blamed the poor state of the road on

the often and Contynuall drifts and droves of Cattell [and the] frequent passages of Waynes Carts and Carriadges [which made the road] soe fowle, full of holes, sloughes, gulles & gutters . . . and soe dangerous that noe Coatch Carte nor horse loaded cane almost passe that waie.

The problem here was a combination of heavy traffic, flat clayey ground, the lack of a local supply of stone or gravel for repair, and the small size of the villages whose job it was to repair this section of a major route.

Various legal remedies were tried; some parishes were fined or ordered to contribute funds, rates were levied, whilst elsewhere the number of days of statute labour was doubled (from 6 to 12 a year). One of the parishes with the worst problems was Standon, 6 miles (10km) north of Ware, through which the Great North Road ran. The parish had been the subject of formal complaints about the road eleven times between 1621 and 1661, and it had appealed to Parliament for assistance on several occasions. Finally, the first turnpike act (allowing the collection of tolls) was granted in 1663, and duly put into effect. It essentially provided the local justices with an extra way of raising money to repair the 15

miles (24km) from Wadesmill to Royston. The wording of the preamble to the act is typical of many later ones:

Whereas the ancient High-way and Post-Road . . . by reason of the great and many Loads which are weekly drawn in Waggons . . . as well by reason of the great Trade of Barley and Mault that Cometh to *Ware* . . . is very ruinous and become almost impassable . . . and for that the ordinary course appointed by the laws and statutes . . . is not sufficient for the effectual repairing and amending of the same . . .

Several subsequent bills were defeated, but it is not clear why. It may have been because of local or parliamentary opposition, because tolls were seen as a new and unwelcome tax, or even because no further improvements to the road repair system were needed. It was not until 1695 that further turnpike acts came into force. By this time, the problems in some parishes had become acute, and the number of new turnpike acts began to increase steadily from 4 in the 1690s, to 10 in the 1700s, 22 in the 1710s, and 46 in the 1720s.

A major innovation introduced between 1706 and 1714 was that turnpikes became autonomous of the justices, and were run by independent appointed unpaid trustees or commissioners. They were empowered to erect gates, appoint surveyors and collectors, collect tolls, demand statute labour (or its monetary equivalent), mortgage the tolls, elect new trustees and undertake road repairs (Albert, 1972). Eventually the turnpike tolls replaced the parish labour system entirely on most lengths of the major roads. Turnpike trusts were originally intended to be temporary bodies which would be dissolved when the roads had been improved; thus their original acts usually lasted for only 21 years. But renewal became a standard occurrence and was made automatic in 1835; many renewal and amendment acts altered the mileage covered by the trusts.

The establishment of the turnpike *system* was essentially a local affair, and thus the network grew piecemeal. It was not planned by central government in any way, but by people who had an interest in improving individual sections of roads, thus facilitating travel and trade. In order to create a turnpike, a group of interested local landowners, farmers, manufacturers, town councils or traders would put forward a bill to Parliament. For example, the list of subscribers to the Standedge-Oldham turnpike of 1797 included 36 clothiers, 8 merchants and 6 gentlemen. The bills usually stated that the reason for the proposal was that the road could not be kept in repair, but occasionally it was suggested that real benefits would also be gained.

Objections could be made, perhaps by those who thought they might be disadvantaged (for example farmers, drovers, carriers or traders living elsewhere). Opposition was not uncommon at the start of the eighteenth century and the grounds included landowners deliberately allowing a road to fall into disrepair so that it could be turnpiked and tolls charged. Elsewhere objectors thought that only a short section of a proposed turnpike needed repair, or that a new turnpike would compete with existing turnpikes or navigations. However, only five bills were actually defeated up to 1750, though a further 48 disappeared during the parliamentary process. Some opposition was violent rather than legal, with local rioting and the occasional destruction of gates. After 1714, most bills were successful, and the early intermittent riots ended with those in Leeds in 1753. They began again with the 'Rebecca Riots' in South Wales in the early 1840s, sparked off by hard times and the erection of too many tollgates; the biblical reference is to the seed of Isaac's wife, who should possess the 'gate' of her foes. The word 'turnpike' originally referred only to the tollgate.

Lists of new turnpike acts are given in Albert (1972), and Pawson (1977), but rather annoyingly Albert's work is restricted to England, and Pawson's list ends in 1800. Another problem is that their brief descriptions often give little idea of the route(s) involved; their 'Kirby-in-Kendal to Sedbergh, etc' and 'Sedbergh roads' of 1762 in fact include three separate roads. Moreover, many renewal acts included powers for new lengths of road, and the occasional disturnpiking of others but these are not listed by Albert or Pawson. The only complete set of acts is in the House of Lords Record Office, and renewal acts are usually only available in manuscript. Any local study will require detailed research among all the acts for each road.

The precise date of a turnpike act has little more than legal importance, and is only a relatively unimportant moment in a much longer process. It tells us only that an act had been passed for a length of road which presumably had heavy traffic, and was in need of improvement. It is certainly not the date when any part of the road was actually improved, as repairs would not have begun until some time later, and would continue throughout the life of the trust.

The turnpike network

By the middle of the eighteenth century, London was clearly the centre of the turnpike network, with 13 main routes leading to the rest of the kingdom (Albert, 1972). These roads led to Berwick (the Great North Road), Manchester (two routes: via Derby or Coventry), Hereford (two routes: via Abingdon or Oxford), Bristol, Worcester, Birmingham, Shrewsbury, Chester, Harwich, Dover and Chichester (Fig. 77). The total length of these English through routes (excluding the duplicated sections) was 1564 miles (2500km); only 113 miles (182km) had not been turnpiked by

ROADS TURNPIKED
— between 1663 and 1727
— between 1728 and 1751
···· after 1751

0   miles   50

Buckton Burn
(······Berwick-upon-Tweed)
Newcastle
Darlington
Boroughbridge
Manchester
Doncaster
Buxton
Little Drayton
Chester
Cranage
Newhaven
Lawton
Tittensor
Nottingham
Stone
Derby
Grantham
Shrewsbury
Loughborough
Shifnal
Lichfield
Leicester
Stamford
Wansford Bridge
Coleshill
Wednesbury
Meriden
Birmingham
Coventry
Market
Harborough
Alconbury
Worcester
Daventry
Northampton
Stratford
Newport
Pagnall
Royston
Warmington
Hereford
Broadway Hill
Woburn
Colchester
Harwich
Buckingham
Chipping
Norton
Hockliffe
Stevenage
Gloucester
Woodstock
Chelmsford
Oxford
Wendover
Ware
Cirencester
Fyfield
Barnet
St. John's Bridge
Abingdon
Beaconsfield
Uxbridge
Chippenham
Henley-on-Thames
LONDON
Bristol
Marlborough
Reading
Maidenhead
Blackheath
Bath
Cherhill
Newbury
Pountfield
Kingston-
upon-Thames
Rochester
Canterbury
Hindhead
Dover
Petersfield
Portsmouth
Chichester

1751. This is a remarkable achievement, given that each route had been turnpiked by many different trusts. The average length of road under each of these trusts was about 14 miles (23km), while the longest single length (north of Newcastle) was only 51 miles (82km). In 1751 the main roads to Exeter and Norwich still remained largely unturnpiked and there were still no turnpikes at all in Cornwall, Devon, Dorset or Wales, only 7 miles (11km) in Westmorland and 13 miles (21km) in Norfolk. To the north the Scottish system was just starting to develop, though not at first connected to the English turnpikes.

Not all turnpikes led towards London; many provincial centres were also attracting turnpike networks. Some trusts were centred on particular towns, and were responsible for several of the roads leading into them. The first such trust was for Bath in 1707, followed by acts for Ledbury, Worcester, Tewkesbury, Bristol, Warminster and Leominster before 1730. Town trusts were evidently a West Country fashion. Some turnpikes were made for purely industrial reasons; examples include the road from Liverpool to the coal mines at Prescot (1725), as well as various roads around Birmingham in the late 1720s. Even remote Whitehaven created four turnpikes to bring coal and other goods into the town in its Harbour Act of 1739; at the time there were no other turnpikes within 80 miles (130km), the nearest being at Preston. This sort of development was an extreme case of the disjointed development that was the norm. In most areas a coherent network began to emerge, though Whitehaven had to wait until 1762 before it had a turnpike connection to the rest of England (Fig. 78).

Not every road needed turnpiking immediately; how soon depended on the

amount and type of traffic as well as on the condition of the road. It used to be thought that most of the early acts were for the 'clayey dirty parts' of the trunk roads near London (Cossons, 1934), but this assumes that geology, soils and topography were the main causes of poor roads. In truth, the sheer amount of traffic, especially near London, was usually the crucial factor. The road from Bawtry to Doncaster, on the other hand, was not turnpiked until 1776. It was described by Defoe as

a pleasant road, and good ground, and never wants any repair.

The fact that there were gaps for many years in the emerging turnpike network does not mean that there were gaps in the road system as a whole. In studying the growth of the turnpike network, it is important to realize that we are seeing the spread of a legal innovation; making a road into a turnpike was essentially a legal change, rather than a physical one. Turnpikes only took over existing roads which needed improvement, there was little building of new roads at this period. Some acts were never implemented, and it is always wise to check before assuming that an act was translated into road improvements. In Cumberland, an act for a turnpike from Egremont to the Duddon estuary, passed in 1750, is one such (Fig. 78). Moreover, some acts were only partially enforced, as was the case with the Carlisle-Cockermouth-Workington Act of 1753; only the second section was implemented.

The real mania for turnpike acts was from 1751 to 1772, when 389 new acts were passed, compared to only 146 up to 1750. Town centred trusts continued to be popular in the west, whilst the military road from Carlisle to Newcastle was begun in 1751, paid for by the government, though operated as a turnpike (see Chapter 7). The network was growing steadily, covering most of England and Wales, and achieving a

77 *Progress in turnpiking the major routes into London. (This map does not show other turnpikes.)*

TURNPIKE ROADS
— 1739 – 1751
▪▪▪ Not carried out
— 1753
– – – Not carried out
— 1759 – 1767
— Later than 1768
••••• Sands route
▨ Land over 1000ft

0   Miles   5

78 *Turnpikes in Cumbria. The first were those around Whitehaven in 1739, but 1753 saw the passage of six acts of Parliament for this area, totalling about 140 miles (225km). However, two of the acts were not put into effect.*

79 *The progress of turnpiking in the East Midlands; by 1772 a comprehensive turnpike network had emerged. (After Albert, 1972.)*

higher connectivity, as is well demonstrated in the East Midlands (Fig. 79).

The mania also coincided with the early stages of the industrial revolution. At this time populations were increasing, especially in the towns, agricultural production was rising (in a period of high prices) and the parliamentary enclosure of common fields was becoming increasingly frequent. The road improvements were both cause and effect of all these changes; all these sectors of the economy were inextricably interlinked (Pawson, 1977). But some towns stagnated or even declined, many were remote from the new centres of growth and often had poor road connections.

The industrial revolution is often more closely linked with the building of canals, but even when the canal network was complete, most industries still had to rely on roads, even if only as links to the often distant waterway network. The roads were also used for postal services, without which business could not flourish. In agriculture, areas which had been unable to get their produce easily and cheaply to market now found that they could do so, and that demand was increasing. Many areas turned from cattle to arable, whilst others nearer the towns changed from arable to market gardening. One example of this changing agricultural traffic is that the road from Hexham to Alnmouth, turnpiked in 1752, became known as the 'Corn Road'.

The turnpike act mania ceased in 1773, a year in which there were only four new acts,

80   The tollhouse on the turnpike between Todmorden and Littleborough; the tolls are still displayed.

but there was a resurgence in the speculative years of the 1790s, alongside the canal act mania. Some areas had to wait until quite late for their turnpike roads; many of those in industrial Lancashire were implemented only between 1790 and 1810, at the same time as the rapid growth of the cotton industry.

The emerging turnpike network is clearly (and usually accurately) shown on most of the large-scale county maps produced in the closing decades of the eighteenth century, in most cases after the bulk of the turnpikes had been built (Hindle, 1988). These maps are generally at a scale of one inch to one mile (or greater), and they usually depict the turnpikes more boldly than other roads, and show tollgates and mileages (many tollhouses and milestones still survive; Fig. 80).

It is important to consult such maps, as many of the routes first turnpiked are now only minor roads or less, having been replaced by new turnpike roads in the early nineteenth century. A dramatic example is the turnpike from Ingleton to Wensleydale. The original route from Ribblehead followed the Roman road high across Cam Fell to Bainbridge; it keeps at over 460m (1500ft) for 7½ miles (12km), eventually reaching a height of 590m (1935ft), only a few hundred feet lower than the Three Peaks themselves (Figs. 81 and 82). It is still shown on the OS map as Cam High Road, but is now mostly a footpath. An entirely different route further north was built in 1795. It rises to only 438m (1434ft), and then descends north of 'Snays Fell' along Widdale to Hawes.

Towards the end of the eighteenth century, travellers' guides were published in great profusion, catering largely for the demand from those who wished to travel for pleasure. Coach travel on the new roads was becoming much more common, and the Napoleonic Wars meant that travellers went to 'North Britain' rather than across the Alps to Italy. The guides were either in the

81 *The Roman road from Ribblehead to Bainbridge was used by the first turnpike of 1751 (see Fig. 82). This section around Dodd Fell is known as Cam High Road.*

82 *The original turnpike from Lancaster to Richmond (1751) followed the Roman road from Ribblehead high across the hills to Bainbridge (see Fig. 81). Jefferys' map of 1771 shows no sign of the present-day road from Ribblehead to Hawes via 'Widale'. (Reproduced by courtesy of H. Margary.)*

form of lists of places and distances, or in the strip map form invented by Ogilby in the 1670s (see Chapter 5). Some contain much original material, though others were carelessly updated revisions of earlier works; thus they cannot always be relied upon even as evidence for the existence of a road. The classic example is a non-existent road going from Ambleside to Whitehaven via Wasdale Head, over some of the highest ground in England; it first appeared on a small-scale county map in 1749, and was still appearing in guides over fifty years later.

The Postmaster General commissioned a new survey of the roads, and this was published by John Cary as his *New Itinerary* in 1798. He had perambulated some 9000 miles (14,500km) of roads, and it was the first original road survey since that done by Ogilby 120 years before. It describes the routes in written form, and it was extensively copied and added to by other publishers, several of whom used it to update their texts, maps or strip maps.

By 1820, there were over 1000 trusts with over 7000 tollgates controlling some 22,000

83 *A comparison of Yates' map of Staffordshire of 1775 (right) with a larger-scale map drawn by Henshall in 1771 shows that the minor road network depicted by Yates is remarkably full and accurate. (Reproduced by courtesy of A. D. M. Phillips.)*

miles (35,500km) of turnpikes (which compares very favourably with the present A- and M-road network of about 31,500 miles (51,000km)). The final turnpikes in England were created in 1836, the very last was from Hastings to Hollington, a distance of less than two miles; such short distances were typical of the later trusts.

At their zenith, turnpikes accounted for almost one-fifth of the total length of public highways, principally the major, heavily-used routes. However, the parishes were still responsible for most roads, a fact that is often forgotten in road histories. Most parishes could maintain these minor roads quite adequately, as they catered largely for local traffic which was generally light both in quantity and weight and it was clearly in each parish's interest to ensure that they were kept in good repair. These roads can

be seen with ever increasing clarity and accuracy on the new detailed county maps (Fig. 83), as well as on the Ordnance Survey maps which were surveyed progressively through the nineteenth century.

Wheeled traffic steadily replaced packhorses on the turnpikes; Manchester's first coach service to London began in 1754, and even Holyhead had a service to London by 1776. Mail coaches were introduced in 1784. The speed of travel for both goods and people improved dramatically. In 1700 it took about 6 days to travel from Manchester to London; this was progressively reduced to just over 3 days by 1750, and to only 28 hours in 1811. Even then, the average speed of coaches rarely exceeded 10 miles an hour.

The cost of moving goods is difficult to ascertain, but it seems to have fallen slightly during the first half of the eighteenth century, and rather more up to 1765. Although costs rose thereafter, they rose less than prices in general; thus the real cost of moving goods continued to fall, and turnpiking continued to prove beneficial to economic growth. This was achieved partly by the increased competition between carriers of both goods and people.

At the start of this century the Webbs (1913) thought that the turnpikes had had little effect on the economy of Britain, seeing them as too indebted and localized to have been of great consequence. The view held today is exactly the opposite: travel times fell, passenger and goods traffic increased in volume, became more regular and reliable, and the turnpikes made it easier to travel throughout the year. The growth in agriculture, industry and towns was certainly not independent of these changes, indeed Pawson (1977) has suggested that

the turnpike system was responsible for initiating many of the social, economic, and geographical changes traditionally ascribed to the railways.

Of course, there were places where improvements were less than satisfactory – some turnpikes were described by contemporary travellers as 'abominable' or worse, especially at the end of the eighteenth century. Arthur Young made frequent references to the state of the roads during his tour of the north in 1771. The road from Kendal to Lancaster was 'Very bad, rough, and cut up', and that from Brampton to Carlisle was 'vilely cut up by innumerable little paltry one horse carts'. On the other hand, he described the road from Kendal to Windermere as

Turnpike; now making. What is finished is as good, firm, level a road as any in the world. I no where remember a better.

Overall, Young described only 28 per cent of the turnpike mileage as 'indifferent', 'bad' or 'vile', whereas 70 per cent of the other (parish) roads merited such descriptions.

The real point is that the road system then, as now, had its black spots as well as its stretches of dry, open highway, . . . This patchiness was perhaps the greatest defect in the turnpike system. (Dyos and Aldcroft, 1969.)

Turnpike improvements

The main reason for the later improvements in the speed of travel was that the techniques of road construction and repair underwent a remarkable transformation during the early years of the nineteenth century. Until then improvements had been very limited; virtually all turnpikes simply took over existing roads, and improved their worst sections. Some turnpikes had first to widen driftways into cartways, enabling wheeled vehicles to travel and to pass each other. There was a tendency to use whatever surfacing materials were available nearby without any specialist knowledge, and other work seldom went beyond digging and maintaining ditches.

The improvement of road building techniques began at the end of the eighteenth century. One of the earliest practitioners was John Metcalf, known as 'Blind Jack of Knaresborough', who was responsible for some 180 miles (290km) of turnpikes in the years between 1765 and his retirement at the age of 75 in 1792. One of his first jobs was to improve the road over Standedge, between Oldham and Huddersfield in 1759 (see pp. 120–4). In the sections of peat bog he first removed the existing vegetation in a strip 13m (42ft) wide and created a camber, he then ordered his workers to pull and bind heather into round bundles and to lay it on the intended road in rows, before covering it with stone and gravel. This high and exposed road needed no further repairs for the next 12 years. His general principles included firm foundations, a smooth convex surface and good drainage ditches. However, Blind Jack was an exception in

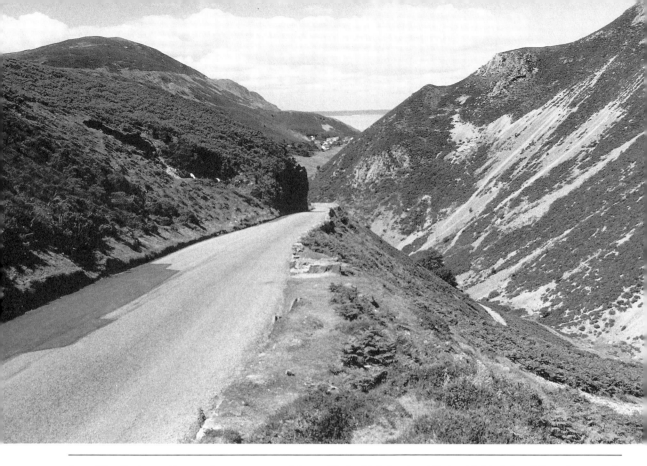

84 *The Sychnant Pass used to carry most of the traffic for Holyhead and Ireland behind the cliffs to the west of Conwy. Anglesey can be seen in the distance.*

the eighteenth century; the major improvements in road construction and maintenance had to await the arrival on the scene of Telford and McAdam in the early years of the nineteenth century.

Thomas Telford was a road builder, much of whose work was in the Highlands of Scotland (see below); his roads were based on firm, hand-set stone foundations, 18cm (7in) deep (in the Roman tradition), overlain with 15cm (6in) of smaller stones. He also paid much attention to reducing gradients, and made his roads wide and straight. His roads were too good for the requirements of his day and such standards of construction were perhaps only needed for the most heavily used roads. They were certainly expensive to build, and his methods were

beyond the financial capacity of most turnpike trusts.

Telford is most often associated with the road from London to Holyhead, especially the Welsh section through the mountains of Snowdonia. Here it had long been the custom to avoid the hills by going down the Conwy valley, and then travelling over the Sychnant Pass (Fig. 84), and along the coast to Bangor on a road perched high above the sea at Penmaenmawr. Travellers sometimes went across the sands to get around the headlands, and even went straight across the Lavan Sands to Beaumaris on Anglesey, instead of taking the ferry from Bangor.

The route through the hills via Capel Curig was described as 'the most dreadful horse-path in Wales' by Pennant in 1759.

85 *Lord Penrhyn's road climbing towards the head of Nant Ffrancon was built in 1791–1800; this section is still metalled.*

86 *Evans' map of 1795 shows the original 'dreadful horse-path' to Capel Curig (half of which is shown by dashed lines), as well as Lord Penrhyn's road which was then under construction (see Fig. 87).*

However, in 1791 Lord Penrhyn decided to build a new road. It ran from his quarry at Bethesda, up the west side of the Nant Ffrancon valley (Fig. 85) and past Llyn Ogwen, finally reaching his estate at Capel Curig in 1800. Both of these early roads are shown on John Evans' map of 1796 (Fig. 86). Lord Penrhyn also built a large hotel (now Plas-y-Brenin) at the end of this road, trying to encourage tourism; his road, however, went no further east. A turnpike act for the whole length from Llandegai (outside Bangor) through to Betws-y-Coed and Pentrevoelas was passed in 1802, and this Capel Curig Trust road was opened in 1808. Most of it was on a new line; it ran up the opposite (east) side of Nant Ffrancon, and then took a new straight route from Llyn Ogwen to Capel Curig, south of the

87 *The four successive routes through the Welsh mountains from Bethesda to Capel Curig. The A5 still follows Telford's final route, though most of the earlier tracks are still roads or footpaths.*

88 and 89 *(Below, left and right) East of Llyn Ogwen, Lord Penrhyn's road was later used by the Capel Curig Trust; most of it is still visible today.*

Afon Llugwy, about a quarter of a mile (0.4km) south of the present A5 (Figs. 87–89).

The heavy traffic of people and post bound for Ireland, plus the increasing number of tourists, meant that the turnpike road, which had poor foundations, deteriorated rapidly. In 1810 Parliament appointed the first of eight select committees to report on the state of the whole of the London to Holyhead road, and Telford prepared a survey of the North Wales sections. Parliament finally voted £20,000 for improvements in 1815, and Telford was appointed as engineer. He soon made recommendations to improve the route, and work began in the same year, with many entirely new lengths. Most gradients were made less than 1 in 20, notably in the ascent of Nant Ffrancon where the old Capel Curig Trust road had had gradients as steep as 1 in 6. Indeed this whole section of the first turnpike had been poorly planned, badly constructed and was often no more than 3.6m (12ft) in width. The six independent Trusts between Shrewsbury and Bangor were consolidated into one in 1819. Telford also improved much of the rest of the road back to London. Despite various recent diversions, the present-day A5 through Wales is essentially the road designed by Telford, and is a fitting monument to his genius (Fig. 90).

John McAdam, the other great road engineer of the early nineteenth century, was principally concerned with the repair and maintenance of existing roads. He proposed that a good road should have a smooth, elastic, slightly convex surface, over a dry sub-soil, without foundations. He said that he would never put stones bigger than 3in (8cm) in diameter in any part of one of his roads, and the surface layer should have stones no larger than 1in (2.5cm) across, laid to a total depth of 10in (25cm). Essentially he was concerned to get good drainage rather than concentrating on

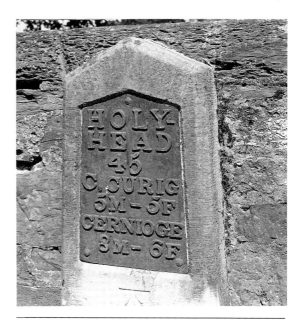

90 *Telford's much improved Holyhead Road (A5) is lined with massive milestones.*

the road bed itself. This technique was not as good as that of Telford, but it was astonishingly simple and effective; it was also much quicker, simpler and cheaper to implement.

He worked first for the Bristol Trust in 1816, and was soon advising trusts elsewhere. By 1823, 147 trusts throughout the country were employing one of his family, or his policies, occasionally with completely new lengths of road being built. In Cumbria, for example, McAdam surveyed a short section of new road north of Penrith avoiding the steep hill out of the town (Figs. 91 and 92), and he rebuilt 10 miles (16km) of the road to Keswick.

On a larger scale he also drew up plans for a new road over the summit of Shap in 1826. This road was one of the more important roads in Britain, being part of the main west coast route from England to Scotland. It was not the original route taken by the Romans, which lies to the east through the Tebay gorge, nor does it follow the other routes to the west which had been used in medieval

91 *A survey done for McAdam in 1825 of a new linking road north of Penrith, designed to avoid the former steep climb out of the town. The fields across which the new road was to run are numbered (see Fig. 92).*

times (over the Nan Bield or Gatescarth Passes). However, by the eighteenth century, Shap had become the usual route. It was used by Bonnie Prince Charlie in 1745; on his retreat to Scotland both he and his English pursuers had great difficulty in

92 *Aerial view of the roads shown in Fig. 91, looking from the junction ('To Salkeld') towards Penrith. The first section of the road above the roundabout is along the line of the original Roman road, whilst McAdam's new link is to the right.*

crossing in the wet conditions. In 1753 the route was turnpiked, and as so often happened in hilly areas, the old packhorse route was simply improved and kept in repair for seventy years before the major improvements of the 1820s (Figs. 93–94).

McAdam designed a completely new summit section, which reaches 416m (1365ft), and includes the long steady climb northwards out of Borrowdale from the new Huck's Bridge. The road which had caused so much trouble in the past was at last capable of taking fast and heavy traffic over this difficult route. For a distance of some 12 miles (20km), the old and new routes run close together, largely independent of each other, the old route still mostly passable on foot, and in two lengths by car (Fig. 95). McAdam's road is still in use today as the A6 though the bulk of the traffic now uses the parallel M6, leaving Shap as a quiet and wide country road.

Back at Standedge, John Metcalf's turnpike, which had merely improved an existing track, was rebuilt along new routes twice, first between 1790 and 1815, and again between 1820 and 1839 (Figs. 96–98)

93　*The first Shap turnpike descending into Crookdale towards Hause Foot Bridge now survives as an impressive footpath.*

94　*Old Wasdale Bridge on the original Shap turnpike, north of Packhorse Hill.*

95 *The original 1753 turnpike over Shap simply followed the existing route. An almost entirely new route was laid out by McAdam in the 1820s, and is still in use today.*

96 *The successive longer but easier routes taken by turnpikes over Standedge between 1759 and 1839; the A62 now follows the final route.*

(Barnes, 1981). Each improvement was better graded than the previous line, and the final (and present) had a long summit cutting; however, it is 20 per cent longer than Metcalf's original route. The

97 *The original line of the Standedge turnpike as laid out by John Metcalf in 1759, viewed from just above Thieves Bridge. The section in the middle distance towards Mount Bar is still in use. The third turnpike runs across the middle ground.*

98 *The junction of the first and third Standedge turnpikes on Harrop Edge; the second can be seen sloping to the right up the hillside in the distance.*

100   *A section of the old Derby to Buxton road north of Brassington, crossing the White Peak near Pikehall.*

99   *Changes in the routes available between Derby and Manchester.*

improvements made throughout this route were considerable, though curiously only a mile of the first route (the summit section) remains unmetalled today. This was

probably the most important route between Lancashire and Yorkshire and as traffic increased, and required easier routes, the Trustees clearly responded accordingly, despite having direct canal competition from 1811. Even before then, canal-borne goods were transferred by packhorse between two ends of the uncompleted tunnel, from Diggle to Marsden, along a track known as Boat Lane (see Fig. 119).

If examples such as the Capel Curig, Shap and Standedge turnpikes seem a little out of the ordinary, it should be remembered that the roads through such difficult terrain were often largely rebuilt along new routes as technology improved. Moreover, as these areas have not been subject to intensive agriculture, the remains of earlier roads often survive. Some examples from less hilly areas will help to balance the picture.

The route from Derby to Manchester has a complex history, for not only have there been local road changes, but the overall route itself has changed three times (Dodd, 1980). The old road in use in the seventeenth century followed the Roman road, via the village of Brassington to Buxton and beyond (Fig. 99). The section from Shardlow to Brassington was turnpiked in 1738, as it was in poor condition, and was described as 'monstrous hilly', despite being in relatively low-lying country. After climbing steeply out of Brassington, the road then ran across the well-drained limestone of the White Peak; this section was adequate for the traffic of the times, and did not require a turnpike act (Fig. 100). A glance at a modern map will show that this route does not even survive as a B road today, though it is joined by the A515 at Hurdlow for the last 6 miles (10km) into Buxton. In fact, the 1738 Act had provided that the road from Derby to Hurdlow via Ashbourne be turnpiked as well; it soon became the normal route, despite being slightly longer. Three successive routes for

the 5 miles (8km) north of Ashbourne were used in the first 40 years of the history of this short section of the turnpike; the route in use here today was built in 1777. All this meant that the road through Brassington ceased to be a through route, and the section from Hulland Ward to Brassington was disturnpiked in 1827 on the grounds that it

led to no City, Town, or place of importance.

North of Buxton, the Roman road, which reaches a height of 457m (1500ft), continued to be used in the first Act of 1724, but towards the end of the century John Metcalf (Blind Jack) laid out a new road now known as the Old Longhill Road. Its summit was slightly lower, at 425m (1394ft), but was immediately followed by a 1 in 6 plunge of 76m (250ft) into a side valley of the river Goyt. The present well-graded road around this valley, which is ¾ mile (1.2km) longer,

101 *The Old Longhill Road descending into a small but deep valley north of Buxton was replaced by a much longer but better graded road in about 1820.*

was built around 1820 (Fig. 101). Beyond Whaley Bridge the first turnpike continued to follow existing roads, climbing twice over the hills to reach Disley and High Lane, where it is joined by the modern A6.

A much greater change to travel between Derby and Manchester had occurred in 1762 when the road from Ashbourne to Leek was turnpiked; travellers could then continue via Macclesfield and Hazel Grove on a much easier route, avoiding the Peak District altogether. When the new main roads of the country were designated in the 1920s, a different route further east through Matlock and Bakewell to Buxton was made into the A6, though the Long Hill survived as the main route north of Buxton until much more recently.

One of the most notorious areas of poor roads in southern England was the Weald, separating London from the south coast (Fuller, 1953). The principal problem was the large outcrop of the Weald Clay, which made both agriculture and travel difficult. Numerous travellers complained of the 'bottomless clay' which produced awful roads, which could by no means be repaired by parish labour. Furthermore, many of these areas were lacking in good road stone, the local gravels and sandstones being too soft. Packhorses provided the best means of transport, but were not suited to carrying the heavy and bulky products of the timber and iron industries for which the Weald was well known.

By 1760 there were six turnpikes from London reaching the coast between Portsmouth and Hastings, though no turnpikes ran east–west. By 1800, the number had increased, and most still ran north–south. Stage coaches could reach Brighton in eight hours, and other resorts including Bexhill, Eastbourne and Worthing were starting to grow as a direct result of these improved roads. But the situation was not as good as a map of these roads might indicate; all were simply existing roads taken over by the trusts, and their condition often left much to be desired. The county agricultural reports make it clear that many were still largely impassable for wheeled traffic in winter, and matters did not begin to improve until after the visit of McAdam to Lewes in 1817. The main north–south roads were soon improved, though some cross-country trusts simply could not afford even to employ a surveyor. As elsewhere it has to be remembered that only a small percentage of roads were turnpiked (though these were almost always the most important). In 1840, the various Surveyors of Highways in Sussex maintained almost four times as much road as did the turnpike trusts.

Turnpikes have not received the detailed local research they deserve. There are several county-level studies of turnpike development and impact; recent examples include those for Derbyshire (Dodd, 1980), Cumbria (Williams, 1975; Hindle, 1984), the Yorkshire Dales (Wright, 1985), Wessex (Wright, 1988) and north-west Wales (Colyer, 1984). There are several older studies, such as those for East Devon (Sheldon, 1928), Nottinghamshire (Cossons, 1934) and the Surrey–Sussex Weald and coastlands (Fuller, 1953). Turnpikes are a topic which the county landscapes histories and local histories usually cover rather inadequately, and sometimes not at all. It would be very useful to have more studies of roads at the local level, such as that by Barnes (1981), which concentrates on the turnpike roads leading over the Pennines at Standedge. An excellent general introduction is given by Wright (1992).

Scotland

There had been a few early tolls on roads in Scotland as early as the 1590s, but the first roads to be turnpiked under the same type of legislation as in England were a number of routes into Edinburgh in 1713. As in England there was a long gap before the next act in 1750. The next three years saw a mini-boom, with turnpikes made from Edinburgh to Falkirk, Glasgow, Stirling and Strathaven, as well as the first stages of the turnpikes to both Inverness (via Queensferry) and England. Glasgow had its own town act in 1753, as did Ayr in 1767. The first turnpike to reach the English border was that from Edinburgh to Coldstream in 1760, followed by the road from Hawick to Scotsdyke (for Carlisle) in 1764, the two roads to Carter Bar (for Corbridge and Newcastle) in 1768 and that to Berwick in 1772. This last link was rather indirect, as the obvious route along the east coast (now the A1) was not turnpiked until 1787. To the north the turnpikes linked in with the slightly earlier military roads of Wade and Caulfeild at Dumbarton, Stirling, Crieff, Dunkeld and Coupar (see Chapter 7). Thus by 1790, the basic network was completed, linking the major towns to each other, to England and to the Highlands.

The single detailed county-level study of Scottish turnpikes deals with the roads of Fife (Silver, 1987). This shows how the network developed from the first act in 1753 which turnpiked the main route north from Queensferry to Perth, plus two side roads. The next act was not until 1790, when a basic network of 17 turnpike roads was created, and the process then continued steadily until the final act in 1842 created the county's 88th turnpike. However, 18 were never implemented and simply remained as statute labour roads.

By the end of the eighteenth century, many roads in the Highlands were in a poor condition, including some of the military roads. From 1803 to 1828, two Government Commissions were charged with building new 'parliamentary roads' and to repair existing roads in the Highlands (Haldane, 1962). This renewed road-building activity

was undertaken to try to develop agriculture and fishing, to help stop emigration and to cure the general distress in the Highlands. Although not turnpikes, these roads fit neatly into the story at this point, first because their engineer was Telford, and second because their construction parallels the rebuilding of turnpikes further south. In legal terms, these roads were very similar to the Holyhead road, which was also financed by Parliament. However, the Highland roads were built more for political and social rather than commercial reasons; the traffic they carried would hardly have begun to pay for the vast expenditure.

Telford drew up two reports by 1803, and by the early 1820s, 892 miles (1435km) of new Highland roads had been made, mostly beyond the line of the Spey valley (Fig. 102). Important routes included the Loch na Gaul road from Fort William to Arisaig (the 'Road to the Isles') and the Laggan road, which allowed traffic to avoid the Corrieyairack Pass. There were two routes to Skye: one was the rebuilding of the Glen Shiel road to Bernera (Fig. 103), plus a branch to Kyle of Lochalsh; whilst the other was the Loch Carron road from Dingwall to Strome Ferry and Kyle of Lochalsh. On Skye, roads led to Armadale, Stein, Uig and Portree, whilst in the far north, there were routes from Bonar Bridge to both Tongue and Thurso. One proposal which was never begun was a new road over Rannoch Moor from Killin to Spean Bridge, intended to replace the military (Old Glencoe) road. Telford also improved and maintained 308 miles (495km) of the old military and other roads, as well as 104 miles (167km) in the lowlands, including sections of the Glasgow–Carlisle road.

Telford's Scottish roads were wide, usually built to a minimum of 6m (19ft); he also insisted that his roads should be surfaced with a thick layer of gravel, which would be best suited to the cattle which formed the principal traffic on the Highland

THURSO
Thurso Rd
WICK
TONGUE
CAITHNESS
SUTHERLAND
Tongue Rd
Dunbeath Rd
Dunrobin Rd
LEWIS
HARRIS
BONAR BRIDGE
Loch Carron Rd
DINGWALL
LOCHCARRON
INVERNESS
BANFF
Strath Glass Rd
Speyside Rd
SKYE
K
Loch Ness
GRANTOWN-ON-SPEY
B
Inverfarrigaig Rd
ALFORD BRIDGE
Glen Shiel Rd
AVIEMORE
Glen Garry Rd
FORT AUGUSTUS
POTARCH BRIDGE
ARISAIG
Loch na Gaul Rd
DALWHINNIE
BRAEMAR
Laggan Rd
FORT WILLIAM
BLAIR ATHOLL
Moydart Rd
Glen Coe
Rannoch Moor
MULL
TYNDRUM
KILLIN
DUNKELD
COUPAR ANGUS
CRIEFF
INVERARY
TARBET
CALLANDER
Loch Lomond
LUSS
JURA
EDINBURGH
ISLAY
GLASGOW
ARRAN
ABINGDON
LOCKERBIE
ENGLAND
CARLISLE

| B | *Bernera* |
| K | *Kyle of Lochalsh* |

—— *Highland roads made and maintained*
---- *Military and other roads improved and maintained*
-- -- *Lowland roads*

0   miles   25

102 *The network of Scottish Parliamentary Roads made or improved by Telford in the early nineteenth century. (After Haldane, 1962.)*

roads. The results were soon felt – trade increased, new coach services started (for example from Inverary to Oban) and London papers could reach Skye in four days. Agriculture was able to prosper in places away from the coast, and there were increased exports, notably of salt fish, grain, whisky and bacon. In order to maintain these roads, some tollhouses were erected, and thus a few of these roads became very similar to the turnpikes further south. Many Highland roads still run along the routes laid out by Telford, and many of his bridges are still in use. His work was a very important contribution to the development of the road network of the Highlands.

Postscript

The 1820s and 1830s were an Indian summer for the turnpikes, but their demise was imminent. The beginning of the end for the turnpikes was to be caused by the building of the railways – the opening of the line over Shap in 1846 caused the revenues on the parallel turnpike to fall from around £240 in 1841 to only £93 in 1852. Tolls soon declined everywhere as the movement of most long-distance goods (everything from cattle to steel) was transferred to the iron

103 *One of the bridges on the Ratagan Pass between Glen Shiel and Bernera, built by Telford in the early nineteenth century, but now by-passed by the 1990 rebuilding.*

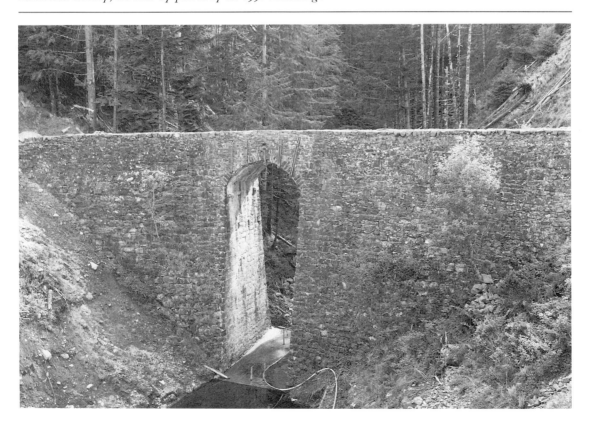

roads. Many trusts were already in considerable debt after the cost of the improvements of the 1820s and 1830s (a total debt of over £8 million in 1838), and the loss of long-distance traffic was a major blow. But the fact that there were many creditors to be paid delayed the dissolution of the trusts. It was also necessary to wait until the railway network was nearing completion before the turnpike system could be dismantled.

Many parishes feared that the burden of road maintenance would once again revert to them, and, as before, this was a particular problem where a road was heavily used. On the other hand, there were parishes which benefited from having a turnpike nearby, but which did not actually pass through the parish; they would get off scot-free if there was no attempt to spread the costs after dissolution. The possible difficulties are well shown in the case of the Ambleside Trust. In 1871 it was estimated that if it were dissolved, one parish would have to raise an additional rate of only ¼d whilst another would be saddled with an additional 6¼d (2½p) in the pound (Williams, 1975).

In the six counties of South Wales, the turnpikes had already been abolished in 1844, and replaced by road boards in each county. This was a result of the Rebecca Riots in which numerous tollgates had been destroyed during the previous five years. But in the rest of Britain, the government insisted that trusts should pay off their debts in preference to spending money on repairing the roads, and thus the condition of many roads deteriorated during the 1850s and 1860s. Once debts were cleared, trusts could more easily be dissolved, and this generally occurred in the 1870s and 1880s.

Putting these roads back under the control of local highway boards and parishes was hardly a good solution, however, and in 1878 a new act stipulated that all roads disturnpiked since 1870 should be styled 'Main Roads'. Half of the cost of maintaining these roads was to be paid for by the counties, the rest being equally split between the local 'highway districts' and central government. But the Quarter Sessions had to agree to this, and they were often reluctant, especially if there was little through traffic, or if the road was in poor repair. Eventually, most heavily used roads became main roads, including some which had never been turnpiked. In 1888, the whole burden of main road and bridge repairs was passed to the newly-created County Councils, and the upkeep of local roads eventually fell to the Urban and District Councils by the turn of the century.

The turnpike era provides a significant link between early and modern roads, and is particularly important in that, after a gap of some 1400 years, new roads were once again being built and systematically repaired. Most trusts lasted for only just over a century, but during that period, the road system was revolutionized; a national network of well-surfaced through routes was created out of the chaotic system which had preceded it. By the end of the nineteenth century, the roads had passed into the care of local authorities, but one last dramatic change was still to come, namely the arrival of motor vehicles, and this made yet more changes inevitable. But before dealing with the modern era, it is necessary to go back briefly to look at the impact which parliamentary enclosure had on roads in the years around 1800.

9 Enclosure roads

Many western and northern parts of Britain have long had fields enclosed by walls or hedges, and their number and size have increased or decreased in response to changing population levels and to the demand for farmland. In 'Midland England', however, large open fields seem to have been established around the new villages early in the medieval period. But the enclosure of individual fields was not unknown here too, either within the large open fields, or as part of the process of bringing new land, which had previously been waste, moor, wood or fen, into cultivation.

By Elizabethan times many open arable fields were being enclosed by landowners who wished to use the land to pasture sheep or cattle instead. Whole villages were sometimes depopulated, and there was local and even national opposition, but still the process continued. In some areas farmers and landowners agreed to enclose fields; the process was carried out piecemeal, often only a few fields at a time. Thus by the middle of the eighteenth century, large areas of Britain were enclosed. New walls and hedges divided the fields, but most roads had changed little. These areas are often referred to as 'old enclosures'.

From about 1760, a new type of enclosure was becoming common, achieved by Act of Parliament, though the initiative was always taken by local landowners. This parliamentary enclosure was driven by the wish to raise agricultural production in order to feed the ever-growing population, especially in the towns. The growth of industry and the Napoleonic Wars both added to the demand, and the turnpikes made it easier to get the produce to market. The process involved replacing the remaining inefficient open fields by enclosed fields, though by the end of the century, common and waste land was also being extensively enclosed by this method.

Most parliamentary enclosure took place during the reign of George III (1760–1820). Two-thirds was enclosure of open field, and one-third of common and waste. The sheer extent of this process is astonishing; 21 per cent of England was enclosed by Act of Parliament, with many counties in Midland England having far higher figures:

Over 50% enclosed: Oxford, Cambridge, Northampton, Huntingdon
40–49% enclosed: Bedford, Leicester, Yorkshire ER, Rutland
30–39% enclosed: Lincoln, Nottingham, Buckingham, Berkshire, Warwick, Norfolk
21–29% enclosed: Wiltshire, Middlesex, Cumberland★, Gloucester, Yorkshire WR★, Derby, Westmorland★

★ Counties where more than half of the enclosure was of common and waste.

Parliamentary enclosure was not so

important in those areas which were already largely enclosed, or where much land was unsuited to intensive arable farming – as well as northern and western areas of England, this included large parts of Wales and Scotland. Nevertheless, many lower-lying areas of Wales and Scotland were enclosed at this time; most of this enclosure was of common and waste land, as there were few open fields in these areas. Roughly a quarter of Cardigan's and Radnor's common and waste was enclosed in the nineteenth century, but overall, perhaps only 4 per cent of Wales was enclosed between 1793 and 1815.

Much has been written about the history of English enclosure, for example Turner (1980) and Yelling (1977), though that for Scotland and Wales has yet to be published. Rather less has been written about the impact of enclosure on the landscape, and in particular about the changes to local road systems; indeed, consideration of enclosure roads is totally missing from several of the regional road histories. This is all the more surprising in view of the fact that the face of so much of England was totally altered by these Acts of Parliament. This is another topic crying out for detailed local research.

The process of enclosure began when a group of local promoters placed a bill before Parliament; it might then be opposed, but it usually became an Enclosure Act, allowing them to proceed. They would then nominate Commissioners who had the task of re-allocating the land holdings according to the *value* of the land involved. One of their first jobs was to appoint a surveyor to draw up a written survey and a plan of the area as it was, so that each person's holdings could be measured, and the new layout was then planned. The end result was a document called the Enclosure Award, a large book detailing the new holdings, with the surveyor's new plan appended; the plan of the old landscape rarely survives, especially from before 1830 (Hindle, 1988).

Each landholder would usually have his or her holdings amalgamated into one or more fields, and the Commissioners would arrange for new hedges or walls to be built. In the process, the surveyors usually redesigned the whole landscape, starting with the roads. Some enclosure awards set aside areas for quarrying, either to provide stone for building field walls instead of planting hedges, or for road surfacing material. Enclosure was not cheap, and the new roads were usually the major single item. At Ulceby (Lincolnshire) the Commissioners' account totalled almost £11,300, of which the cost of roads, drains and other works was just short of £6500 (Russell, 1982).

An interesting problem is to try to find out what the old landscape and the old roads were like. They can be reconstructed in various ways: there may be a map of the parish drawn before enclosure; the surveyor's map of the old landscape may survive; or, failing that, it may be possible to read between the lines of the enclosure award, though this last method is better for revealing the old field boundaries rather than the roads. A few of the old roads may still survive, especially where they pass through old enclosures; some were improved and thus retained, but many others which ran across the new fields were either deliberately 'discontinued', or have simply become disused, and may or may not survive. Thus many very old tracks and field paths were deliberately obliterated by the process of enclosure, while others have simply been ploughed out of existence since then. Some of the most detailed work has been done for parts of Lincolnshire, where the Russells (1982–87) have painstakingly reconstructed the pre-enclosure landscape of numerous parishes, and contrasted it with the new landscape. This allows us to see the remarkable changes which the enclosure surveyors wrought (Fig. 104).

The most obvious feature on the

104   *The enclosure of West Ashby (Lincolnshire); outside the old enclosures, the whole landscape of roads and fields was newly created. (Reproduced by courtesy of R. Russell.)*

enclosure award maps, as well as on the ground today, is the regularity and orderliness of these new landscapes (Fig. 105). In particular, straight lines and deliberate (often right) angles abound in the field boundaries and in the road layout (Fig. 106). Occasionally the old roads were widened and straightened, and this can sometimes result in right-angled bends, marking where the old road went round the heads of the medieval furlongs. But in most cases completely new roads were laid out, they were typically both straight and wide. They share their straightness with Roman roads, but are easily distinguished from the latter, as they never lead to Roman sites and are rarely more than a few miles long. Hoskins (1955) sums up very clearly how

105   *Typical enclosure landscape north of Penrith; the main road is the A6, on top of the Roman road to Carlisle.*

106 *An 18m (60ft) wide enclosure road in West Ashby (Hemingby Middle Road, see Fig. 104); the modern strip of tarmac is wide enough only for a single vehicle.*

107 *The parish boundary between Fulletby (in the foreground) and Greetham is shown by the change in width between the hedges (from 18 to 12m, 60 to 40ft), and by the slight change of direction.*

much they differ from older country lanes:

There is none of that apparently aimless wandering in short stretches, punctuated by frequent bends, going halfway round the compass to reach the next hamlet or village . . .

Typical widths are 9, 12, 15 or 18m (30, 40, 50 or 60ft). This allowed enough room for the traffic of carts and wagons to go around any obstruction, following the long-standing tradition that travellers had the right to diverge from a difficult section of road, even if they had to trample crops; at least now the crops were safe.

Where enclosure roads reach the parish boundary, there is sometimes a slight bend. As each parish was usually enclosed at a different date, the bend represents the work of two different surveyors who had each put in a straight road (perhaps of different widths) from their village to the boundary. North-east of Horncastle the neighbouring parishes of Greetham and Fulletby were enclosed 18 years apart; at the boundary there is a change of road alignment, and the

108 *The two redrawn enclosure maps for Fulletby (top) and Greetham show the result of enclosure at different dates on the road connecting them (see Fig. 107). (Reproduced by courtesy of R. Russell.)*

period (that is an 'old enclosure'), its roads were not normally improved, and the difference may well be very obvious, with the new enclosure roads suddenly degenerating into the old narrow and twisting lanes. Within the parish of West Ashby (Lincolnshire), the new enclosure road to Hemingby narrows suddenly and becomes a very obviously old sunken lane as it passes through an old enclosed area for quarter of a mile (near Far Thorpe), before widening abruptly back to the standard width of 18m (60ft) as it regains the new enclosures (Russell, 1985). Further north, on the shores of the Humber estuary, in the parish of South Killingholme, enclosed in 1777–8, the difference between the old enclosures with their narrow winding lanes, and the new landscape of enclosure is even more marked (Fig. 109) (Russell, 1982).

Enclosure roads nearly always run through the parish, and only rarely run along the parish boundary as they were designed to give access from the village to the new fields, as well as to lead to the next village. Originally, many enclosure roads were partly surfaced with whatever stone or gravel was available, though others were not. In the East Riding of Yorkshire, the surfaced strip was usually 5–6m (18–20ft) wide, whatever the width between the walls. Any main roads or turnpikes through an enclosure area were usually left largely unaltered, though they might have been widened or straightened.

In a few places fields have encroached on the roads since the date of enclosure. An early example of this was noted north of Cartmel (Lancashire) in 1872, when James Stockdale, the village's historian, noted that one section of the road to High Newton

width changes from 12 to 18m (40 to 60ft) (Fig. 107). The redrawn sketch of the enclosure map (Russell, 1985) shows the difference between the old and new roads very clearly (Fig. 108). If for some reason the roads did not meet up exactly at the boundary, a double bend might result.

If part of the parish, or the adjacent parish, had been enclosed piecemeal before this

appears exceedingly narrow, as if it had never been made of the same width as the lower part of the road; but on closer examination the original walls will still be found standing on each side at the full statute width.

109 *At Killingholme, enclosed in 1777–8, the difference between roads through the old and new enclosures is very clearly seen. (Reproduced by courtesy of R. Russell.)*

Here, hedges had grown up in front of the original walls. In most places the hedges or walls are still far apart, and a narrow strip of tarmac runs forlornly between them.

In the Wolds of the East Riding of Yorkshire, a series of changes affected roads in the 5 miles (8km) between Butterwick and Burton Fleming (Allison, 1976). The villages were enclosed at various dates between 1769 and 1840, and one result was to move the main east–west road away from the low-lying ground near the Gypsey Race, while two entirely new roads linked this road to the village of Foxholes (Fig. 110).

There are exceptions to all of this – in some parishes, the enclosure surveyors kept the old roads, but simply altered the fields. This happened at Cartmel, under the Act of 1796, where the roads still weave their way through much the more regular fields. The roads here were not widened either, and still remain to this day at the local 'statute' width of 6m (20ft). However, some were surfaced; one was to be

covered ten feet [3m] wide with broken stones not bigger than a goose's egg, . . . nine inches [23cm] in thickness on the crown of the road.

More frequently, winding drove roads were confined between the new walls without being straightened (Fig. 111).

Occupation roads are in many ways similar to enclosure roads; many were created in the nineteenth century as higher ground, typically on the northern fells, was enclosed and apportioned. A good example can be seen on the fells to the south of Dent where what is now called the 'Green Lane' was created in 1859 as part of the process of dividing up the former common grazing land. It connected the Barbondale and Deepdale roads out of Dentdale, and it curves around the hills for 5½ miles (9km), rising from 285m (935ft) to 525m (1720ft). In addition, two new tracks were also created, leading straight back into the valley;

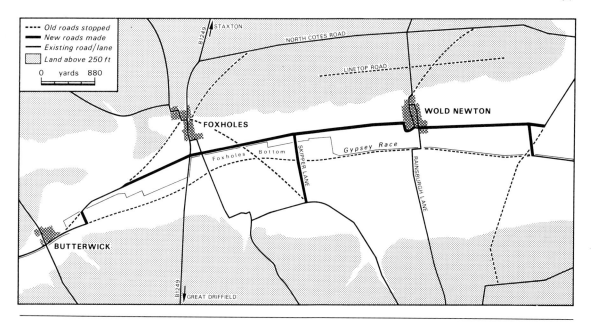

110 *Enclosure at various dates from 1769 to 1840 near Butterwick (Yorkshire) completely altered the road pattern. (After Allinson, 1976.)*

all of this was designed to improve access to the newly-enclosed moorland.

The impact of parliamentary enclosure on the economy in the years around 1800 was very important, but its impact on the landscape of England was particularly dramatic. One-fifth of England was re-designed, and probably close to one-fifth of the mileage of country lanes dates from this period. Many enclosure walls and hedges may have been removed in the last 20 years, but the enclosure surveyors' roads remain largely intact, sometimes hampering modern traffic as much as they helped transport two hundred years ago. Parliamentary enclosure provided the last major change to the road network of many parts of Britain, alongside which the twentieth-century motorways represent only a small additional mileage.

111 *An enclosed drove road near Orton (Westmorland) winds its way through the later enclosed fields.*

10 The modern era

The start of the modern era in the history of British roads was the result of the ever-increasing amount of traffic, the changing nature of that traffic and the need for a more efficient transport system. By the end of the nineteenth century, the railway network was virtually complete, providing the backbone of such a system, but there was still the problem of getting goods to and from the stations, usually on horse-drawn carts along roads whose surfaces could not cope with the continuing increase in traffic.

The arrival of the bicycle also had an effect, though unlike most earlier traffic on the roads, it was used mainly for pleasure. It appeared in something like its present form, complete with pneumatic tyres, in the 1880s, and by the turn of the century was to be seen in great numbers. Cyclists demanded better road surfaces than the gravelly strips which then existed, though there was little actual improvement as a result of their complaints. On the contrary, there was much opposition to the flood of cyclists, because they alarmed horses and pedestrians, raised dust and went as fast as 12 miles (19km) an hour. One result was that lights (for all vehicles) and bells (for bicycles only) were made compulsory by 1888.

But it was the automobile that was to change the road system out of all recognition. Early attempts at mechanized transport in the form of steam traction engines led to the introduction of a speed limit of 4mph (6.5kph) in 1865, and the infamous man with a red flag had to walk in front of such vehicles in order to warn oncoming riders and horses. However, the petrol engine was introduced in 1894, and the 'man and flag' act was repealed two years later. Cars were soon able to travel much faster than any previous traffic, and as they steadily became more numerous, they began to destroy the road surfaces which had been built for the much slower coaches and wagons. To make matters worse, motorbikes and then motor omnibuses weighing up to 7 tons also soon appeared. By 1912 there were over 175,000 motor vehicles in England and Wales.

At the turn of the century, most of the main roads were built to the standards laid down by McAdam, but were often only wide enough for two wagons to pass; minor country roads were often much worse, with numerous deep ruts and potholes. Many roads were too steep or tortuous for the new motorized traffic. The option of trying to restrict vehicles was not taken, and instead road improvements were begun, partly due to the lobbying efforts of groups such as the Roads Improvement Association, which had had its origins among the early cyclists. Cars had to be licensed from 1903, a speed limit of 20mph (32 kph) was set in 1906, and in 1909 came the introduction of taxes on pleasure motor vehicles and on petrol.

The major single improvement was the sealing of road surfaces with tar, aptly named after McAdam (even though he had died in 1836). The application of 'tarmac' was well under way by 1910, and by 1930 there were few lanes which had not been tarred. Tarring made roads waterproof and more durable, by binding the surface stones it reduced the damage done by the traffic. It also reduced the large amount of dust which was raised from roads without tarmac.

The administration of English highways was still in the hands of almost 2000 separate local authorities, but in 1909, a Road Board was set up that was the first tentative step towards the introduction of a national highway policy. It encouraged councils to improve road surfaces by ensuring that there was a solid crust of crushed stone, which was rolled smooth and tarmaced, and also by widening, straightening or levelling roads where required. At the start, this assisted only the 23,500 miles (38,000 km) of roads in England and Wales maintained by the County Councils, rather than the 95,000 miles (153,000 km) under the control of the Rural Districts. The Webbs (1913) record that

the Great North Road from London to Carlisle [sic] is in the hands of seventy-two separate Authorities . . . varying from the tiny Rural District Council . . . up to the Council of . . . the largest . . . Boroughs.

But none of these authorities had the power to make new roads.

The Ministry of Transport was set up in 1919, and one of its first achievements was to complete the classification of roads. In 1920, central government began contributing towards the cost of road maintenance. The years between the two World Wars saw the building of the first bypasses, to avoid congestion in towns throughout the country. It was a novel notion that roads should go around towns rather than pass through them. New arterial roads included the East Lancashire Road from Liverpool to Manchester, and the road

between Glasgow and Edinburgh. Many stretches of other important roads were also rebuilt. As early as 1932, Anderson was bemoaning the loss of many old roads:

All over the country the roads are being reconstructed . . . Now there is scarcely a patch of genuine old road left in England.

But this road-building activity ceased at the end of the 1920s because of the financial crisis. Governments started to use road taxes for other purposes during the 1930s, and the roads were underfunded.

The first nationally administered route network came with the Trunk Roads Act of 1936; the intention was to provide a 'national system of routes for through traffic'. The bulk of the work was never begun because of the start of the war. From 1899 to 1936 the road mileage grew by only 4 per cent, and virtually no attempt was made to construct roads capable of carrying fast traffic. There was no national road policy, simply because the numerous road authorities remained largely autonomous. In addition, there was little initiative from the Ministry of Transport, which had only limited powers. The road programme failed totally to keep pace with the growth of motor traffic.

In 1938, Sir Charles Bressey pointed out that there was a bottleneck on average every mile all the way from London to Birmingham. In London he pointed out that:

[the] transport machinery is already overstrained . . . Congestion in innermost London has already reached such a pitch that, on main routes through the city, vehicles are often reduced to a slow walk . . . there is great reluctance to break with the past and embark upon a vigorous modernization of a decrepit highway system designed for horse transport.

Fifty years on, and despite numerous road improvements, little has changed, and speeds are no better.

After the war, the government made almost 3700 miles (5950km) of roads into trunk roads, which were to be their direct responsibility. But the Ministry of Transport seemed to think that a few local

112 *Two extracts from Ordnance Survey 25-inch plans show the creation of suburban roads alongside the railway only a few miles north of Manchester.*

improvements plus traffic control schemes would solve all traffic problems. It was not until the 1950s that the government really started to increase expenditure on roads, though by then there was a 25-year backlog of neglect. These road improvements, together with the new motorways, led to great government optimism. In 1960 the Minister of Transport said that 'the problem of getting from city to city will not be a problem in about five years' time'. The problem within towns was better appreciated, and was the subject of the Buchanan Report, *Traffic in Towns*, written in 1963.

Since the 1960s there have been numerous schemes to improve roads, whether by widening, straightening, creating dual carriageways, improving junctions and building bypasses or ring roads. Priority has clearly been given to inter-city routes and to the main roads within urban areas, but virtually all roads have been improved to a greater or lesser extent. Yet the number of vehicles, and of cars in particular, has kept increasing, and at a faster rate than the increase in road space. It is clear that traffic expands to fill the road space available, and the consequences in terms of congestion and falling traffic speeds are obvious to all road users.

At the start of the 1990s the total mileage of Trunk and Principal roads is almost 30,000 miles (48,300km). But the total length of minor roads is much greater; there are almost 70,000 miles (113,000km) of B and C roads, plus over 120,000 miles (190,000km) which are unclassified. Much of the old minor network is still much as it was a century ago, but many new minor roads have been created, most are unclassified suburban roads (Fig. 112). The evidence for all this change is voluminous, whether in the minutes and records of government departments and local councils, or in the much more easily accessible map record. Ordnance Survey maps at all scales

have been regularly revised, and survey dates are usually given; often smaller-scale maps have been reissued with only the main roads altered.

Motorways

The single greatest change to the road system in the twentieth century has been the creation of motorways. The notion of such totally new roads was being aired in the early 1920s. Belloc (1923) said that private interests (the railways) had defeated a scheme in which new arterial roads would have linked the main centres of population. New motorways were actually being built in Italy, Germany and the USA in the period between the two World Wars, yet nothing along these lines was done in Britain, despite plentiful labour supplies due to the high levels of unemployment. The Institution of Highway Engineers and then the County Surveyors' Society put forward detailed proposals in 1936 and 1938, and the post-war government finally announced definite motorway proposals in 1946 (Fig. 113). It was proposed to start work in about 1951; an enabling act was passed in 1949, but it was not until 1956 that the first motorway construction was actually begun.

The whole process of building a motorway is long and complicated. First the need for a particular length of motorway has to be justified (usually on grounds of existing congested roads), and money has to be made available. Then a route has to be chosen and a public enquiry held, the road is then designed, the land is purchased (often by compulsion), and compensation terms agreed, before construction can begin. In addition, many existing features, including other roads and footpaths, have to be altered.

The first short stretch of the M6, opened in 1958, was little more than a restricted access bypass for the A6 around Preston.

113   *Three sets of proposals for the British motorway system. It is interesting to compare these plans with what has now been built.*

But in the following year the first major length of motorway was opened, namely the section of the M1 from just outside Watford to a field near Crick in Northamptonshire, where it linked up with the A5 (i.e. the Roman Watling Street!). These new roads were intended to allow rapid and safe long-distance movement, they increased capacity, had limited access points, excluded pedestrians, cyclists and various slow vehicles, and did not interfere with existing roads during their construction; furthermore it was hoped that they would leave the 'old roads' for cyclists and local traffic. All this was thought to be better than widening or dualling the existing main roads.

In the space of thirty years, the motorway network has grown dramatically, and is still growing. The completion of London's 'Motorway Box', the M25, has been the most expensive and controversial scheme to date. Known unkindly as London's 'orbital car-park', it is already extremely heavily used, often congested and is in dire need of improvements. The latest major addition to the national network, the 48 miles (77km) of the M40 from Oxford to Birmingham, partly designed to relieve pressure on the 30-year-old M1, was opened in 1991. The total length of motorways at the start of the 1990s was 1852 miles (2980km), with a further 170 miles (274km) of new motorway planned or under construction. In addition, almost 600 miles (965km) of existing motorways are to be widened in the early 1990s (Trunk Roads, 1990).

Despite the 1946 plan, and various

subsequent proposals, there is a distinct feeling that the network has grown without a detailed master plan. On the one hand there are some stretches which are grossly overloaded, while others see much less traffic. There are clearly also certain routes which have not yet been provided with motorway links: these include Manchester to Sheffield; Birmingham to Southampton, as well as from the Midlands to East Anglia (first proposed in 1936). Nevertheless, the recent development of towns, housing and industry has been radically affected by the location of the motorways; proximity to a motorway access point or junction can prove a valuable asset to some, and a nuisance to others.

An alternative strategy has been to upgrade certain existing roads, rather than building totally new ones; the classic example is the A1/A1(M) from London to Tyneside which was made into a mixture of motorway and dual carriageway beginning in the early 1960s. By 1990, 75 out of the 260 miles (121 of 418km) were already motorway, and the whole route is to be upgraded to motorway standards during the 1990s. A similar idea to improve the A4 instead of building the M4 was rejected many years ago and the A4 still survives largely intact.

Roads and landscapes

During the 1970s and 1980s it became fashionable for residents (and others) to oppose any new road schemes in their area, almost as a matter of course. Everyone wants to be able to drive their car from one place to another, just so long as a new road does not go through their own backyard, or cross the breeding ground of the lesser-spotted-whatsit. Moreover, many people see any newly proposed road as nothing more than a potential scar on the landscape. There have been a number of *causes célèbres*.

An early example of a major campaign to alter a road proposal occurred in the early 1970s when it was proposed to widen and improve the A66 in order to link the then new M6 at Penrith to the towns of the West Cumberland coast. This route has a long history, having seen turnpike improvements in the nineteenth century, and further work between the wars. It had already been entirely rerouted between Penrith and Penruddock, and west of Keswick it went along the shore of Bassenthwaite Lake rather than its original route over the Whinlatter Pass. The proposals largely kept to the then existing route, using the disused railway in places, adding bypasses around Keswick and Cockermouth. Numerous individuals, as well as bodies such as the Countryside Commission and the Lake District Planning Board objected to the proposals, and an alternative route keeping outside the National Park was suggested, following the B5305 almost to Wigton, and then the A595 to Cockermouth (Fig. 114). This route was slightly longer, but the cost would have been virtually the same. Many people thought that a fast road designed to serve the coastal towns was not appropriate for a road through a National Park, on which people prefer to travel more slowly, enjoying the views rather than getting from one place to another as fast as possible.

The road has now been built through the Lake District and, with careful roadside planting, is already starting to blend into the landscape. This is clearly an emotive issue, as many people see roads (especially new ones) as blots on the landscape. But to anyone standing on the Lakeland fells, there are numerous man-made eyesores such as car-parks, caravan sites, quarries, regimented coniferous forests, reservoirs with 'draw-down' shorelines and even the towns themselves, alongside which the sweeping curves of the new road are but a minor intrusion (Fig. 115).

Early in 1990, the government announced

114 *Proposals for an improved route from the M6 to the West Cumberland coast made in the early 1970s. The A66 route, through the National Park, has now been built (see Fig. 115).*

its intention to build the missing section of the M3 near Winchester across Twyford Down, rather than tunnelling beneath it. The predictable local (and national) outcry followed immediately, even though the scheme involves digging up the present bypass and returning it to nature. This last event is a very unusual step indeed; very rarely in the long history of roads has a perfectly good road been taken out of use deliberately.

Only a few months later, a leaked draft of a possible route for the Greater Manchester Western and Northern Relief Road immediately raised a hornets' nest of opposition, even before a preferred route had been selected. This plan intends to build a new motorway from the M6 at Knutsford to the M62/M66 junction. Across north Manchester it is planned to run closely parallel to the existing M62 (which is itself being widened to four lanes each way). The new road would run through housing and recreational areas, including the Croal–Irwell Valley.

Perhaps the most obvious gap in the present network is between Manchester and Sheffield, which are the two largest

115 *The still-new A66 bypassing Keswick. It is a moot point whether the A66 or Keswick itself is the worse blot on the natural landscape. The now disused railway track, partly alongside the new road, was once no doubt as intrusive as the new road, but it has blended into the landscape. (Photo by courtesy of Peter Thornton.)*

conurbations not yet connected by a motorway. But whether it would now be possible to build such a link across the Pennines (using either the Woodhead or Snake Pass routes, and probably involving tunnelling) is very doubtful. We have now almost reached the stage where it is difficult to imagine the existing motorway network being built at all under present conditions. Projects such as the Settle-Carlisle Railway line or the magnificent route of the M6 through the Lune Gorge would surely be successfully opposed were they to be proposed today. It may well be that the planning laws will themselves have to be bypassed in order to build some future routes; a precedent has already been set by some of the works connected with the Channel Tunnel, where public enquiries were avoided.

To those who decry new roads as scars on the landscape: Scott-Giles (1946) said that a new road might be

crude maybe, at first, but pleasanter . . . where time has mellowed and nature dressed it.

And he hoped that there would still be

separate paths for those who travel by cycle or on foot; and here and there, curving off the great artery, a side way leading to lesser roads and thence, by devious but unbroken routes, to quiet by-ways where the leisurely may still wander, and even to age-old paths where wheels may not go.

It is indeed possible to argue that roads can add to landscapes, in the same way that canals and railways have done. Bridges, viaducts and aqueducts are impressive features, and few would suggest that the Pontcysyllte aqueduct or the Ribblehead viaduct should now be pulled down on aesthetic grounds. It is worthwhile remembering that many railway schemes were objected to in the nineteenth century, yet their structures are now jealously guarded. Ruskin opposed the building of

Monsal Dale viaduct, but the now disused structure is protected by a preservation order. No doubt the Tinsley viaduct carrying the M1 past Sheffield, or the Barton high-level bridge taking the M63 over the Manchester Ship Canal will stand as monuments to the road architecture of the late twentieth century.

Roads themselves can become important features in the landscape; the two curving levels of the M6 as it passes through the Lune Gorge (Fig. 116), the dramatic crossing of the Pennines by the M62, and the way in which the M5 climbs the ridge south of Bristol are all good examples. James Drake (1969), a noted County Surveyor responsible for many of the early motorways in Lancashire, demonstrated his enthusiasm clearly:

The building of a motorway is sculpture on an exciting grand scale, carving, moulding and adapting . . . earth, rock and minerals into a finished product, which must be both functional and pleasing to the eye, as well as economical and durable.

Footpaths

Many tracks and lesser routes have gone out of use, been ploughed out or built over. Nevertheless, there are some 140,000 miles (225,000km) of public footpaths, bridleways and byways in England and Wales. The basic legal distinction between these three types of right of way is that footpaths are for walkers only, bridleways may also be used by cyclists and horse riders, whilst byways (often green roads or other old roads) are open to all traffic, including wheeled vehicles. In addition there are 'roads used as public paths'. The situation in Scotland is somewhat less precise, partly because there is much more open country than exists south of the border; the Scottish Rights of Way Society was formed to defend footpath access in Scotland.

The M6 curving its way through the Lune Gorge, adding an architectural layer to the landscape.

Definitive footpath maps should now exist for all counties of England and Wales, and for some in Scotland, they should be kept up to date by the local highway authority. However, several counties have yet to complete their maps. Ordnance Survey maps (1:25,000 and 1:50,000) also show rights of way, though they are always at least a little out of date, and thus not quite as reliable as the definitive maps. The 1:25,000 scale maps are, in fact, called 'Pathfinder' maps; they show rights of way in green. There is no shortage of published footpath guides, as a visit to any good bookshop will show. The maintenance of all these tracks is normally the responsibility of the County Councils, though they may delegate the job to District or Parish Councils, or to the National Park authorities. In practice this can sometimes lead to confusion, with each leaving the job to the others.

The idea of creating long-distance footpaths or National Trails, was made possible by an Act of 1949. These paths are in many ways the footpath equivalent of the motorways, except that they are largely based on existing rights of way. The first to be designated was the 270 mile (435km) long Pennine Way; originally suggested in 1935, it was finally 'opened' in 1965 (Stephenson, 1969). It has since been followed by many more, with several following old routes, including the

Ridgeway Path (see Chapter 2), the Norfolk Coast Path (which includes the Peddar's Way, see Chapter 3), the North Downs Way (Pilgrims' Way, see Chapter 4) and the West Highland Way (partly drove road, military road and turnpike, see Chapters 6, 7 and 8). Others are purely modern inventions. Offa's Dyke Path, for example, follows the eighth-century defensive line, while the Pembrokeshire Coast Path forms the backbone of a National Park. The longest is the South-West Peninsula Coast Path, which totals 515 miles (830km); it already has unusual literary associations (Wallington, 1986).

There are now many other long-distance routes; the 1990 edition of the *Long Distance Walker's Handbook* lists over 340. Most are described officially as Recreational Paths, and their origins are often due to the efforts of ramblers, local authorities or voluntary groups and their creation and management may be supported financially by the Countryside Commission. These paths vary enormously in length. Some are quite long,

---

117   *The towpath of the Manchester, Bolton and Bury Canal at Nob End has become part of the local footpath network.*

---

such as the 190 mile (306km) Coast to Coast Path from St Bees to Robin Hood's Bay, though many are much shorter. An example not in the handbook is the Irwell Valley Way which runs for 30 miles (48km) close to the river from the centre of Manchester to its source above Bacup. Even shorter routes are referred to as Local Walks or Parish Paths; some are specifically designed as circular day walks, with the car driver very much in mind. Of course, even on the long routes, most people simply walk short sections – the number of people going for day walks on parts of the Pennine Way far outnumbers the few who actually walk its entire length.

A recent phenomenon is the 'Challenge Walk', in which walkers are challenged to walk a particular route of 20 or 25 miles (32 or 40km) on a specific day; badges or certificates may be available on completing these walks. They tend to encourage speed rather than leisure, and may also contribute to footpath erosion. Perhaps the best known (and permanently established) one is the 24 mile (39km) Three Peaks Walk which takes in the summits of Ingleborough, Whernside and Pen-y-Ghent, starting and ending at a local cafe.

Finally, there are canal towpaths (most of which are usable, even if the canal is not), and the entirely new footpaths created where abandoned railway lines have been turned into walks or nature trails (Fig. 117).

A problem encountered by many of these routes is that it is difficult and often expensive to create new rights of way and those planning new routes try to use existing rights of way wherever possible, as many landowners are very reluctant to grant new access routes across their land. There is an obvious potential conflict between recreation and farming, and footpaths can also hinder conservation and preservation of the countryside; but more often, landowners simply wish to keep people off their land at all costs. Thus some recreational paths take rather odd routes, perhaps going round three sides of a square on existing metalled roads where a new footpath would have been better.

Rights of way may also be extinguished if they are no longer needed, though local voluntary groups usually object to any such proposal by a landowner. A special case is where land is used by the Ministry of Defence; here routes have been lost on a temporary or even permanent basis, often due to the use of live ammunition. Notable areas where this has happened include large areas of Salisbury Plain, Dartmoor and south Pembrokeshire, as well as numerous small sites throughout the country. Perhaps with the likely decrease in the size of the military in the 1990s, some of these areas and paths will be returned to the public.

Large tracts of Britain have no rights of way at all, and access to such areas is at the whim of the owners; this is especially true in Scotland. Many landowners simply accept customary usage, but a few actively seek to restrict access. A good example is to be found on Casterton and Leck Fells, near Kirkby Lonsdale, beneath which lies the largest cave system in Britain. There are no rights of way across the fells, other than the two roads to the highest farms, and both owners have placed severe restrictions on those wishing to visit the numerous caves. This is all a far cry from the situation in Sweden where the public has the right to roam virtually anywhere as long as no damage is caused. Of course Sweden is twice the size of Britain and has a much smaller population, but the rights of access there are in sharp contrast to those in this country.

Groups such as the Ramblers' Association have taken a strong view on preserving and using footpaths, and the RA is actively campaigning for general public access to all land in open country. In September 1990, it organized a 'Forbidden Britain Day' on which five areas with special access problems were highlighted. In the areas they

chose, access was being refused, restricted or threatened: by a shooting syndicate in the Peak District; landowners in the North York Moors; two noble lords (in the New Forest and the Chilterns); and by the Brecon Beacons National Park Authority!

The ordinary walker is often faced with problems such as blocked or overgrown paths or barbed wire, as well as farmers who do not reinstate paths within two weeks of ploughing or who (legally or illegally) keep certain breeds of bulls in fields crossed by rights of way. A Countryside Commission survey of 1988 found that over half the rights of way in England and Wales were impossible to follow without the use of a map; 68 per cent were not signposted where they left a road (as required by law), and 17 per cent were difficult or impossible to follow, even with a map. And all this assumes that the average walker can in fact read a map in the very precise manner required to locate and follow a footpath which is not clear on the ground.

Despite all these difficulties, walking is now without doubt the most popular form of countryside recreation, and the increasing number of footpath signs reflects the greater leisure use of these old rights of way (Fig. 118). But certain footpaths, so long neglected as a recreational resource have now become seriously over-used. Some of the tracks up Snowdon and many of those in the Lake District have become scars on the landscape, and have had to be reinforced with stone chippings, rebuilt or even re-routed. One of the most drastic solutions has been the construction of several miles of wooden walkways to replace an ever-widening peaty morass on various paths of the Three Peaks Walk (for example the direct descent from Pen-y-Ghent to Horton, and from Ingleborough to the Hill Inn). A very different solution has been adopted in the case of the Lyke Wake Walk across the North York Moors, which once reputedly saw over 40,000 walkers in a single year. It

118   *A variety of footpath and right of way signs.*

has now been removed from many lists of walks and from maps in an attempt to reverse the damage.

Another problem is the increasing use of mountain bikes; they may be ridden on bridleways and byways, but their use on footpaths is illegal, as it is on the hills themselves (unless the owner has given express permission). It is rather curious that these bikes are named after part of the landscape where they should not be used! But rather more serious is the use of motorbikes and four-wheel drive vehicles on unsurfaced tracks (Fig. 119). The use of these vehicles may or may not be illegal,

depending on the legal status of the track involved, but a great deal of damage can be done to ancient tracks in a very short time, making them difficult or impassable for other more traditional users.

The future

It is always dangerous to try to predict what may happen in the future. Writing as recently as 1971, Hindley thought that by the end of the century, moving pavements and transporters would be in general use, freight and people would travel by pipelines, electric cars would be universal, town cars would be silent cubes, the movement of all town traffic would be controlled by computers, and that vehicles would be hovercraft or use magnetic suspension rather than wheels. Instead, the private car is clearly here to stay; it offers so many advantages that it is unlikely to be surrendered voluntarily in the foreseeable future. It has already changed so many attitudes, and has affected the growth and planning of numerous aspects of life.

Our roads are becoming ever more congested, and traffic speeds are falling, especially in towns, largely because of the ever-increasing level of car ownership which has continued to grow faster than the available road capacity. Solutions to this problem involve either improving the infrastructure of roads, or trying to reduce the amount of traffic, or both. But supply and demand are not independent of each other – building a new road obviously creates more capacity, but it also generates new traffic.

Improving roads has so far this century been controlled by the level of government spending. The current strategy is to build new roads and motorways, and to widen existing ones. At worst this will provide only a short-term set of better routes between traffic jams. And there are limits to

119 *A motorbike rider on the second Standedge turnpike which now runs across National Trust land.*

the number of new roads and improvements that can be made; Britain already has more tarmac per square mile than any other country in the world apart from Belgium. Matters are worst in towns where there is the very real danger of destroying much of the urban fabric to make way for the private car. Outside the towns, it has recently been proposed that some new roads might be privately financed; these would be toll roads for those who could afford to use them, essentially marking a return to the turnpike system.

Reducing the demand might be achieved by such measures as charging people more for simply owning a car, discouraging the issue, use and subsidy of company cars, charging road users for travelling (either by increasing fuel taxes or by road pricing),

reducing the number of commuters by persuading people to work from home via electronic communications, trying to encourage people to go back to using public transport (whether bus, tram or rail), and getting more goods traffic off the roads and back on to the railways. For many years governments have been extremely reluctant to invest in the railways, partly justified by the curious way in which rail schemes are costed. British rail investment is the lowest in western Europe, reflected in the Government's refusal in 1990 to fund a high-speed link to the Channel Tunnel. The net result has been an emphasis on building new roads, though certainly not enough to keep pace with the increasing demand.

Roads in towns and throughout the south-east present the most obvious problems, but the main inter-urban routes are also becoming increasingly congested, as they are in other less obvious areas. Twenty million people live within a three-hour drive of the Lake District, thanks to the completion of the M6 in 1971. On popular weekends and especially on Bank Holidays, the problem has become acute, and the southern Lakes has become totally full of cars on a number of occasions – in 1989 the Police twice closed the area to incoming traffic. Here there are strong objections to building more or wider roads, and thus the only solution appears to be to control the demand. An entry fee has been suggested, as has making visitors park outside the Park (perhaps near Kendal) and travel in by bus. Others hope that the prospect of congestion will keep visitors away, but this hardly helps the local residents. The problem is neatly summed up in two of the aims of the National Park which are in conflict with each other, namely to provide access, and to preserve the landscape; it is extremely difficult to promote such an area and encourage people to visit it without destroying something of what the visitors have come to enjoy. At worst the Lake District may have to be redesignated as a National Car Park.

Nationally, there is at present no overall coherent national transport strategy, and the strategy for roads is short-sighted to say the least. In the past the gut reaction has been simply to give more money for road building when problems became serious, partly prompted by the need to keep car-owning voters happy. But there is also a very strong 'roads lobby' at Westminster, which seems to include The Department of Transport, often cynically referred to as The Department of Roads. The solutions thus far adopted are usually belated, piecemeal, inadequate and often strongly affected by public opinion; they frequently do little more than shift the congestion further down the road. Such a reactive strategy tends to ignore most of the fundamental issues, but very soon a government will have to face up to the transport problem as a whole. It may well be that global issues such as the greenhouse effect and the need to control exhaust emissions may yet help to bring about a coherent transport policy by restricting the use of cars. Nevertheless it is clear that, whatever happens in future transport planning, roads will remain as the main element of the transport system of Britain:

we only know that so long as men travel by land the road will go on. (Scott-Giles, 1946.)

Bibliography

Aitken, R. (1990) *The West Highland Way*

Albert, W. (1972) *The Turnpike Road System in England, 1663–1840* (Cambridge)

Aldcroft, D. H. (1975) *British Transport since 1914*

Allison, K. J. (1976) *The East Riding of Yorkshire Landscape*

Anderson, R. M. C. (1932) *The Roads of England*

Bagshawe, R. W. (1979) *Roman Roads* (Princes Risborough)

Barnes, B. (1981) *Passage Through Time* (Saddleworth)

Belloc, H. (1910) *The Old Road*

Belloc, H. (1913) *The Stane Street*

Belloc, H. (1923) *The Road* (Manchester)

Bettey, J. H. (1986) *Wessex from AD 1000*

Bonser, K. J. (1970) *The Drovers*

Cochrane, C. (1969) *The Lost Roads of Wessex* (Newton Abbot)

Colyer, R. (1976) *The Welsh Cattle Drovers* (Cardiff)

Colyer, R. (1984) *Roads and Trackways of Wales* (Ashbourne)

Copeland, J. (1968) *Roads and their Traffic, 1750–1850* (Newton Abbot)

Cossons, A. (1934) *The Turnpike Roads of Nottinghamshire*

Crofts, J. (1967) *Packhorse, Waggon and Post – Land Carriage and Communications under the Tudors and Stuarts*

Crosher, G. R. (1973) *Along the Chiltern Ways*

Dodd, A. E. and E. M. (1980) *Peakland Roads and Trackways* (Ashbourne)

Drake, J. (1969) *Motorways*

Dunn, M. (1986) *Walking Ancient Trackways*

Dyos, H. J. and Aldcroft, D. H. (1969) *British Transport – An Economic Survey from the Seventeenth Century to the Twentieth* (Leicester)

Fenton, A. and Stell, G. (1984) *Loads and Roads in Scotland and Beyond* (Edinburgh)

Fiennes, C. (1982) *The Illustrated Journeys of Celia Fiennes* (ed. C. Morris)

Fuller, G. J. (1953) 'The development of roads in the Surrey–Sussex Weald and coastlands between 1700 and 1900' *Institute of British Geographers: Transactions & Papers* 19

Godwin, F. and Toulson, S. (1977) *The Drovers' Roads of Wales*

Gregory, J. W. (1931) *The Story of the Road*

Groves, R. (1972) 'Roads and Tracks' in Gill, C. *Dartmoor – A New Study* (Newton Abbot)

Haldane, A. R. B. (1962) *New Ways Through the Glens* (Newton Abbot)

Haldane, A. R. B. (1973) *The Drove Roads of Scotland* (Newton Abbot)

Hemery, E. (1986) *Walking Dartmoor's Ancient Tracks*

Herbstein, D. (1982) *The North Downs Way*

Hey, D. (1980) *Packmen, Carriers and Packhorse Roads* (Leicester)

Hindle, B. P. (1984) *Roads and Trackways of the Lake District* (Ashbourne)

Hindle, B. P. (1988) *Maps for Local History*

Hindle, B. P. (1989) *Medieval Roads* (Princes Risborough)

Hindle, B. P. (1990) *Medieval Town Plans* (Princes Risborough)

Hindley, G. (1971) *A History of Roads*

Hooke, D. (1977) 'The Reconstruction of Ancient Routeways' *The Local Historian* 12

Hoskins, W. G. (1955) *The Making of the English Landscape*

Jackman, W. T. (1916) *The Development of Transportation in Modern England* (Cambridge)

Jennett, S. (1971) *The Pilgrims' Way*

Jennett, S. (1976) *The Ridgeway Path*

Johnston, D. E. (1979) *Roman Roads in Britain* (Bourne End)

Jones, B. and Mattingly, D. (1990) *An Atlas of Roman Britain*

Jusserand, J. J. (1889) *English Wayfaring Life in the Middle Ages*

Kerr, J. (1991) *Highland Highways: Old Roads in Atholl* (Edinburgh)

Long Distance Walker's Handbook (1990)

Margary, I. D. (1948) *Roman Ways in the Weald*

Margary, I. D. (1973) *Roman Roads in Britain*

Maxwell, I. S. (1976) *Historical Atlas of West Penwith* (Sheffield)

Moir, D. G. (1975) *Scottish Hill Tracks – Old Highways and Drove Roads* (2 vols.)

Munby, L. M. (1977) *The Hertfordshire Landscape*

Pawson, E. (1977) *Transport and Economy – the Turnpike Roads of Eighteenth-Century Britain*

Peel, J. H. B. (1976) *Along the Green Roads of Britain*

Porter, J. (1980) *The Making of the Central Pennines* (Ashbourne)

Raistrick, A. (1978) *Green Roads in the Mid-Pennines* (Ashbourne)

Richardson, A. and Allan, T. M. (1990) 'The Roman road over the Kirkstone Pass: Ambleside to Old Penrith' *Transactions of the Cumberland & Westmorland Antiquarian & Archaeological Society* 90

Robertson, A. E. (1947) *Old Tracks, Cross-country Routes and 'Coffin Roads' in the North-west Highlands* (Scottish Mountaineering Club Journal)

Robinson, B. (1986) *The Peddars Way and Norfolk Coast Path*

Russell, E. and R. C. (1982) *Landscape Changes in South Humberside* (Hull)

Russell, E. and R. C. (1983) *Making New Landscapes in Lincolnshire* (Lincoln)

Russell, E. and R. C. (1985) *Old and New Landscapes in the Horncastle Area* (Lincoln)

Russell, E. and R. C. (1987) *Parliamentary Enclosure and New Lincolnshire Landscapes* (Lincoln)

Scott-Giles, C. W. (1946) *The Road Goes On*

Sheldon, G. (1928) *From Trackway to Turnpike . . . East Devon* (Oxford)

Silver, O. (1987) *The Roads of Fife* (Edinburgh)

Steane, J. (1974) *The Northamptonshire Landscape*

Stephens, W. B. (1981) *Sources for English Local History*

Stephenson, T. (1969) *The Pennine Way*

Storer, R. (1991) *Exploring Scottish Hill Tracks* (Newton Abbot)

Strong, L. A. G. (1956) *The Rolling Road*

Taylor, C. (1979) *Roads and Tracks of Britain*

Taylor, W. (1976) *The Military Roads in Scotland* (Newton Abbot)

Thomas, J. M. (1970) *Roads before the Railways, 1700–1851*

Timperley, H. W. and Brill, E. (1983) *Ancient Trackways of Wessex* (Shipston-on-Stour)

Toulson, S. (1983) *The Moors of the Southwest; 1 Exploring the Ancient Tracks of Sedgemoor and Exmoor*

Toulson, S. (1984) *The Moors of the Southwest; 2 Exploring the Ancient Tracks of Dartmoor, Bodmin and Penwith*

Toulson, S. (1980) *The Drovers* (Princes Risborough)

Trunk Roads, England: Into the 1990s (1990) (HMSO)

Turner, M. (1980) *English Parliamentary Enclosure*

Viatores, The (1964) *Roman Roads in the South-East Midlands*

Wallington, M. (1986) *500-Mile Walkies*

Watkins, A. (1925) *The Old Straight Track*

Webb, S. and B. (1913) *English Local Government – the Story of the King's Highway*

Williams, L. A. (1975) *Road Transport in Cumbria in the Nineteenth Century*

Wright, G. N. (1985) *Roads and Trackways of the Yorkshire Dales* (Ashbourne)

Wright, G. N. (1988) *Roads and Trackways of Wessex* (Ashbourne)

Wright, G. N. (1992) *Turnpike Roads* (Princes Risborough)

Yelling, J. A. (1977) *Common Field and Enclosure in England*

Index